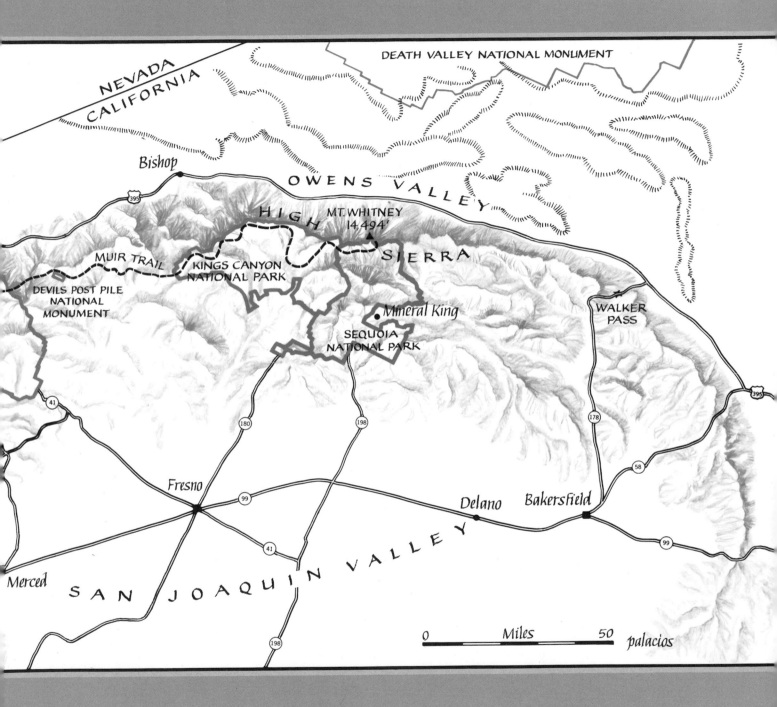

DEATH VALLEY NATIONAL MONUMENT

NEVADA
CALIFORNIA

Bishop

OWENS VALLEY

HIGH
MT. WHITNEY
14,494'
SIERRA

MUIR TRAIL
KINGS CANYON
NATIONAL PARK

DEVILS POST PILE
NATIONAL
MONUMENT

Mineral King

WALKER
PASS

SEQUOIA
NATIONAL PARK

395

178

58

Fresno

99

Delano
Bakersfield

41

99

Merced
SAN JOAQUIN VALLEY

198

0   Miles   50   *palacios*

SIERRA NEVADA
400-MILE MOUNTAIN

SIERRA ALBUM

SIERRA ALBUM

by Paul C. Johnson

DOUBLEDAY & COMPANY, INC., GARDEN CITY, NEW YORK

Foreword

This pictorial scans selected highlights in the story of man's attempt to tame a wild mountain world, the towering Sierra Nevada. As a kind of visual anthology, this book is by no means the complete and final word on so vast a subject, but, hopefully, the dramatic and bumptious story that it reveals will contribute to the appreciation and preservation of California's grandest natural resource.

The author wishes to express gratitude to the staffs of the Sierra Club, National Park Service, United States Forest Service, California State Parks System, and California State Library for direct assistance in turning up fresh graphic materials, and to award nosegays to Judith Whipple for design collaboration and to Joan Storey for serendipitous research.

A word of special appreciation is due to the devoted Sierrans, Francis P. Farquhar and Einar Nilsson, who introduced the author to the Sierra and wittingly, or unwittingly, inspired the creation of this book.

Paul C. Johnson
San Francisco

by Paul C. Johnson:

SIERRA ALBUM · PICTORIAL HISTORY OF CALIFORNIA · SAN FRANCISCO · YOSEMITE · CALIFORNIA · GRAND CANYON

as Supervising Editor, Sunset Pictorials:

BEAUTIFUL CALIFORNIA (1963 Edition) · THE CALIFORNIA MISSIONS · NATIONAL PARKS OF THE WEST · LOS ANGELES

Contents

The Four-Hundred-Mile Mountain

The Sierra Nevada is, roughly, one enormous mountain, four hundred miles long and forty-five miles wide, sculptured into chasms, elevated into peaks and thirteen-thousand foot crests, clothed with forests, and paisleyed with wildflowers. The range stretches from the Tehachapi Mountains at the south to the beginning of the volcanic Cascade Range near Lassen on the north. On the west, it slopes gently down into the Gold Country foothills; on the east, it drops precipitously into Owens Valley.

The range of fire-born granite was formed by a massive upthrust that tilted the block toward the coast, producing the thirty-five-mile gradual slope on the west and the steep, ten-mile descent on the east. The range crests in a hundred-and-fifty mile strip of treeless granite peaks, troughs, and bowls known as the High Sierra or "The Range of Light," a poetic name bestowed by naturalist John Muir that captures the sparkling character of the alpine world of white granite, snow, and cloudless skies.

The Sierra is California's weather factory and the life-giving source of its water supply. The high-crested massif blocks the moist air flowing off the ocean, causing it to rise and release rain and snow on the mountain.

The nation's deepest snowpack (887-inch record) builds up through the winter, layered by succeeding storms that alternate with spells of bright sunny weather. The earth-warmth of the granite and the shy winter sun melt the snow slightly, not enough to dispel it, but enough to keep the streams running through the winter. The storms dwindle by late spring and the snow melts rapidly, swelling the rills that run down to join the rushing rivers.

Comes then the ambient summertime with clear, dry, hot days and cool nights. Occasional storms cannonade among the granite peaks, scattering lightning bolts and drenching localized areas with fat raindrops.

The challenge of the Sierra summits rouses the daredevil in men. Here, pioneer photographer W. H. Jackson takes his precarious stand in 1895 on the Overhanging Rock, three thousand airy feet above Yosemite Valley.

Mountains and Men

This is a story of a century of confrontation between man and the Sierra Nevada—"the most divinely beautiful of all the mountain-chains"; of the foolish and noble, venal and selfless actions inspired in man by contact with this alpine world; and of the marks that men have left behind on the not-so-eternal granite.

Man has approached this mountain world in many moods—reverently, angrily, rapaciously. The first white men to sight the range, the Spaniards, viewed it from a distance in 1772 and named it on a map in 1776. They referred to it as *una gran sierra nevada*—"a great snow-covered range"—but did not explore it, considering it impenetrable. Later, a Spanish punitive expedition, in pursuit of horse-stealing Indians reached the western base of the range in 1806, and discovered the Kings and Merced rivers and Mariposa Creek, but they too had no interest in attempting a mountain foray.

Americans, seeking furs or heading for settlement in Mexican California in the 1820s and 1830s, were thus the first white men to cross and explore the Sierra. The early emigrant parties regarded the range as a dreaded obstacle across their path to the Promised Land. They

9

Who would ever dream that you could drive a Dodge motor car along the trunk of a fallen tree? Tourists had to come and see for themselves and pose for a verifying snapshot.

Loggers swelled with pride after felling giant sequoias, the world's largest trees. Their axes rang in the Big Tree groves for three decades and were not stilled until the 1890s.

were followed by the forty-niners, who fanned out over the Sierra foothills, riddled the mountainsides with mine pits, skimmed off in a decade the gold accumulation of eons, and then moved on. Loggers, shepherds, and cattlemen crowded into the mountains to serve the miners and their successors. They pre-empted the Sierra as their private domain, regarded authorities as poachers, and denuded meadows and forests.

Arrayed against these predators appeared a philosophical rainbow of conservationists, ranging from those who favored controlled exploitation of the Sierra's bounty to those who believed the wilderness should be untouched. Whatever the shadings of their beliefs, the conservators united against the wanton abuse of the Sierra and fought through to fruition a number of epoch-making laws that have saved and restored some of the Sierra heritage.

The very immensity of the Sierra landscape, its Jovian scale, has exalted and stretched the imaginations of both rascal and saint. Practical men matched the mountain's challenge with astounding feats of engineering and construction, building railroads, dams, flumes, and alpine

Many a soggy camper has come to suspect that the rainlessness of the Sierra summers is a myth.

highways by rules improvised for the job. Even the despoilers were inspired to invent ingenious ways of bringing their plunder out of the wilds to the market place.

The tall peaks inspired men to risk their necks on ascents never before attempted by bipeds. The open miles of glistening granite-land lured other venturers to explore the unknown, blaze fresh trails, and stretch their legs along the roof of the North American world.

The Sierra's lakes, rivers, and scenic spectacles drew legions of vacationers and tourists of the "more succulent type," to borrow John Muir's wry phrase, to the resorts and campgrounds. As early as the 1860s, camping parties were sleeping out under the Sierra's rainless summer sky. Even the deep snow of winter, a slushy nuisance to those who lived in it, brought winter sports to the Sierra beginning in the 1850s.

Who now remembers the time when fish were so plentiful that a catch such as this was cause for good natured derision?

In less than a hundred years, men have brought the Sierra to terms. They have not always done so with wisdom or even common sense, but the story of the conquest is leavened with adventure, high spirits, and no little derring-do. Even when they were cutting down

trees dating back to the age of Exodus, the loggers glowed with innocent pride in the skill with which they downed their Goliaths. The story—whether of conserver, despoiler, or the man in between—is a richly human document with more than the usual mixture of good and mischief in motive and action.

So thorough has been the subjection of the Sierra, that the future is already the concern of the present. The pressure of people on the diminishing wilderness, the mobility of unthinking hordes of tourists, and the opening of residential developments in the wilds have transplanted urban headaches to this final, ultimate refuge from the city's ills. Portions of the John Muir Trail are closed because of overuse, flush toilets have been installed on top of 14,494-foot Mount Whitney on the centennial of its first ascent, smog envelops Yosemite Valley and the Tahoe Basin, and the lapis lazuli Lake Tahoe itself is turning sour with algae.

If the restorative values that men seek in the Sierra are to survive there, the next hundred years will provide a sterner test of man's vision and capacity for self-discipline than the lively century glimpsed in this book.

Advance guard of the millions of cars to come, a well-accoutered caravan pauses on a rickety bridge in 1912, girding for an assault on the rutted grades ahead.

Modern ski resorts, such as Squaw Valley, are but the mechanical flowerings of the primitive downhill courses that have served resident Sierrans since the 1850s.

The First Sierrans

In a sense, Indians were the first vacationers in the Sierra. The tribes living in the range occupied well-defined provinces with an upland and lowland. In the summer they moved to the high country to escape valley heat, and with the darkening skies of November, they moved back to lower elevations for the winter.

Through centuries of living with the mountains, the Indians had effected a workable compact with nature that supplied all their needs for food, shelter, and clothing. Expert bowmen, the men hunted deer and smaller game; the women gathered and processed acorns, the Indians' staff of life. They lived in shelters formed of bark; they cooked, winnowed, and trapped game with baskets woven from grasses. The animals and landmarks around them lived in their legends.

The Sierra crest split the tribes into eastern and western groupings. The two traded goods over trails that later became wagon roads and ultimately freeways. Tribes east of the Sierra carried salt from Owens Lake, chunks of obsidian, insect delicacies to exchange for acorns, pine nuts, and baskets from the western tribes.

Generally peaceable, except for the Paiutes in the Owens Valley who were feared by all other tribes, they seldom warred. Their confrontation with the white man came late, in the 1850s, and when it did, it was abrasive and in some areas, lethal. In the foothills, the gold miners overwhelmed them with sheer numbers and swept them aside. But in the higher elevations, where the Indians held a numerical advantage at first, the braves fought desperately to defend their homeland. The Indians of Yosemite fought militia for two years in the 1850s, and aggressive Paiutes engaged Army regulars for several months in the 1860s. Finally subdued, the survivors made a sullen peace with their conquerors and reassembled the shards of their tribal lives.

Here once was the social heart of an Indian camp, the gossip center and nursery school. Here the women gathered to pulverize acorns in the grinding holes pounded deep into the flat rock by generations of hands. Pitted rocks such as these, scattered throughout the oak belt, are all that remain of a once-flourishing Indian culture.

Living off the Land

In a painting as crammed with detail as a museum diorama, Constance Gordon-Cumming depicts an Indian camp in Yosemite ·Valley in 1878. Typical of most of the Sierran tribes, the Yosemites lived in lean-tos formed of slabs of bark and subsisted on game, acorn meal, fish, and insects. The acorns were harvested in fall and stored in silo-like granaries (*in background*). As needed, the nuts were pounded in the grinding stone (*left foreground*) to separate the shell from the kernel, and the meal was then leached in a sand basin (*right foreground*) to remove the bitter tannic acid. When ready, the sweet meal was cooked in boiling water (*center foreground*) heated by red-hot stones dropped into watertight baskets. Note the basketed papoose, conveniently slung from a nearby limb. The animal skins suspended from tree branches account for the absence of men, who were presumably out where they should have been, stalking game. At the time this scene was painted, the Indians had adopted the white man's wardrobe. Women were decorously dressed in blouses and skirts.

Division of Labor

Men hunted; women wove baskets. As John Muir observed, Indian boys learned their marksmanship by shooting at Douglas squirrels. The boy who could hit one of these small and quicksilvery targets was qualified to accompany adult hunters. Indians stalked the wild mountain sheep, once plentiful in the high country. Disguised with a sheep's head, the hunter could often get close enough for a telling shot. Adoption of the white man's rifle made the hunt easier. (*Right*): Baskets woven by the women of the mountain tribes were among the finest in California. This large, handsome basket was reserved for ceremonial use. More practical baskets served as pots and pans, water storage bottles, fish traps, baby carriers.

Trappers and Trailblazers

Honest human greed, milady's fashions, Manifest Destiny, and pure love of adventure were the mixed motives that drove the first white Americans across the Sierra.

First on the scene were fur trappers seeking beaver (of which they found precious few), who rode over Indian and game trails in the 1820s and 1830s. They were followed by scouts sent to spy out the Mexican "mañana land" on the coast and to find ways to reach it overland. Lieutenant John Charles Frémont led two such expeditions across in the dead of winter in 1844–45 and 1845–46, guided by the intuitive tracking of Kit Carson.

The pathfinders reported back that ways had been found to breach California's mountain bastion, and larger parties headed west to scale the redoubt. Where a party of trappers and scouts could travel light and live off the land, the colonizers were burdened with impedimenta for homesteading. The first packtrain to cross, the Bidwell-Bartleson Party, brought women, children, household goods, seed, livestock, and dogs over Sonora Pass in 1841. They were soon followed by the first group to force wagons across the hump in 1844. Once it became known that wagons could cross the Sierra, hundreds of wheeled parties rolled west. The tragic fate of the Donner Party in 1846–47 did not deter the oncoming companies—it merely shifted the favored crossing to the next pass to the south, opened by Kit Carson in 1839.

Crossing the Sierra was a frightful ordeal for most of those who made it; but however terrible the struggle, hundreds succeeded and staked out their reward on the land of Mexican California. War brought California into the United States in 1848—the same year, gold brought the United States into California, as tens of thousands of goldseekers poured over the emigrant trails.

Most unfortunate of the early companies to cross the Sierra, the ill-fated Donner Party was trapped in 1846 by a record snowfall equaled only four times since. The depth of the snow is represented on this memorial at Donner Lake by the top of the masonry pedestal. Even the deep snows of 1969, when this photograph was taken, barely reached halfway to this mark, twenty-three feet above ground.

Breaching the Barricade

Trappers and emigrants approaching the Sierra from the east faced a mile-high wall of rock, broken into a maze of cliffs, crags and impenetrable chasms (*right*). As one exhausted emigrant recorded in his journal, "The rugged side of the mountain is composed of masses of granite. In many places large detached pieces are thrown in the way, rendering it impossible for horses to get a foothold, and in many others it is so smooth that it is as bad for the animals as the more rugged parts." Another emigrant noted that the trail was strewn with "rocks the size of nail kegs, some as big as whiskey barrels, and some as large as sugar hogsheads."

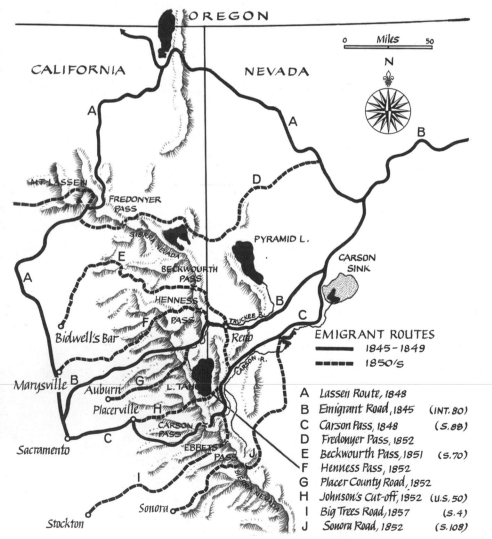

EMIGRANT ROUTES

——	1845–1849
- - -	1850's

A Lassen Route, 1848
B Emigrant Road, 1845 (INT. 80)
C Carson Pass, 1848 (S. 88)
D Fredonyer Pass, 1852
E Beckwourth Pass, 1851 (S. 70)
F Henness Pass, 1852
G Placer County Road, 1852
H Johnson's Cut-off, 1852 (U.S. 50)
I Big Trees Road, 1857 (S. 4)
J Sonora Road, 1852 (S. 108)

The first trappers to enter California avoided head-on assault on the Sierra and detoured around the northern and southern extremes of the massif. First crossing by white men (1827) went from west to east, following roughly the course of present Ebbetts Pass. First east-west crossing, by Joseph Reddeford Walker (1833), passed close to Yosemite's north rim.

The tide of emigration drawn by the lure of gold washed over the Sierra (*left*), following a half dozen major and several minor trails. Travelers struggled up the steep river canyons of the eastern escarpment and down the boulder-choked ravines west of the divide.

Pathfinders

John Charles Frémont (*left*) made two assaults on the Sierra in wintertime, once in 1844 and again the following year. The first crossing took a solid month of floundering that decimated the livestock but miraculously spared the men. Accompanying Frémont as guide, Kit Carson carved his name on a tree in 1844—and this sample (*right*) of early graffiti is carefully preserved in the museum at Sutter's Fort. A small cannon (*far right*) accompanied Frémont's first expedition part way across the Sierra and was finally abandoned in the snow. It was subsequently found—in dozens of places. Of the several pretenders to the role of the true cannon, this fieldpiece celebrating the Fourth of July at Tahoe in 1897 has been acclaimed as genuine by some authorities, vehemently disclaimed by others. Real or spurious, it now ornaments the courthouse lawn at Carson City, Nevada.

Oddly enough, the first crossings of the Sierra were tackled in the dead of winter, with unbelievable hardship, through snowdrifts "from ten to one hundred feet deep." The parties lived off their pack animals as the poor brutes expired.

27

First Wheels over the Redoubt

First wagon trains to struggle across the range made it by brute strength. The wagons were disassembled and hoisted up precipices with block and tackle, inched along with crowbars and the combined muscle of men and oxen. Furniture, clothing, household goods, and hardware were carried on the backs of the men or cached for later retrieval. The first company to cross (1844), led by capable Elisha Stevens (*left*), wrangled six wagons and forty-three men, women, and children over what later became known as Donner Pass (*above*) just before winter set in. This feat encouraged later travelers; a second party rolled over the following year, and the procession of wagon crossings was well launched. Many historians feel that the pass should have been named in honor of Stevens' positive accomplishments rather than the Donners' tragic failure.

The Doomed Donner Party

Of the dozens of emigrant parties that struggled across the Sierra in 1846, the most famous was a loose group of eighty-seven Midwesterners known as the Donner Party, whose gruesome tale of heroism and savagery epitomized the mortal dangers in breaching the mountain barrier in winter. Already late on the road, the party (reduced to eighty-two) arrived at the base of the Sierra on October 31, short of vehicles and livestock. By the time they reached what is now known as Donner Lake, the pass ahead of them was choked with early drifts and snow was beginning to fall. The party built log shelters roofed with wagon canvas and prepared to wait out the storm, but the steady fall of snow, one of the heaviest in California's history, sealed them in camp. After six weeks, a party of fifteen—ten men and five women—set out on snowshoes to bring relief, and thirty-three days later seven emaciated survivors reached Sutter's Fort, sustained en route by the bodies of the eight men who had died. A relief party was promptly organized and sent back to the beleaguered party.

Cannibalism in the Snow

For three and a half months, the Donner camp was a devil's brew of dead, dying, sick, and well. The macabre dependence on cannibalism for survival unsettled even the most stable members of the party, and bitter feuds erupted.

Poignant memento of the terrible ordeal, this tiny doll brought solace to a little girl through the long weeks of tragedy.

When rescuers reached the lake-side camp in mid-February, 1847, the makeshift cabins were covered by thirteen feet of snow. Rescuers herded the survivors to safety in two batches. Of the eighty-two who had reached the Sierra, only forty-seven survived; twenty-one died in the death camps, thirteen on the trail over the summit, one in the Sacramento Valley. Tall stumps (*right*), for many years a landmark at the Donners' camp—five miles northeast of the Donner Lake camp—provided a mute record of the depth of the snow at the time the Donners cut the trees for fuel and cabin building.

The Flood Begins

Scene on the Emigrant Trail,
near Settlements, Nov. 1849.

Once it had been demonstrated that large emigrant parties could cross the Sierra, a tidal wave of humanity converged on California, even while it was still a Mexican province, and swept over the Sierra, leaving a swath of cast-off encumbrances, broken gear, defunct pack animals, and shredded clothing. Fastest time was made by parties on horse or muleback. However, in their long trek they had been mercilessly exposed to sun, rain, or snow, and they could not afford to tarry for members who took sick along the way. Their passage over the Sierra was far simpler than that of the wagon-borne parties, which, though they enjoyed weather protection on the open prairies and could carry their sick and extra water and food, were savagely tested when they faced the Sierra at the tag end of the journey. The exhausted, bickering men had to extract one last climactic effort out of their weary teams to haul the worn-out wagons through the boulder-choked passes. For many parties, the final five-days' push over the Sierra to Sutter's Fort exacted as much energy as the previous month on the open trail.

Roads over the Sierra at the start were no better than trails. As this contemporary print suggests, the traffic was as confused and mixed as the perspective of the drawing itself. Indians, caballeros, Chinese, miners, all competed with covered wagons for the right-of-way.

For decades after the emigrant roads had been abandoned, evidence of the wagons' passing remained. Here, ruts on Donner Pass have eroded into gullies. Nearby, tree trunks still bear scars from passing wheel rims or girdling for rope tows. Stones are streaked with rust stains from the wheels' iron rims.

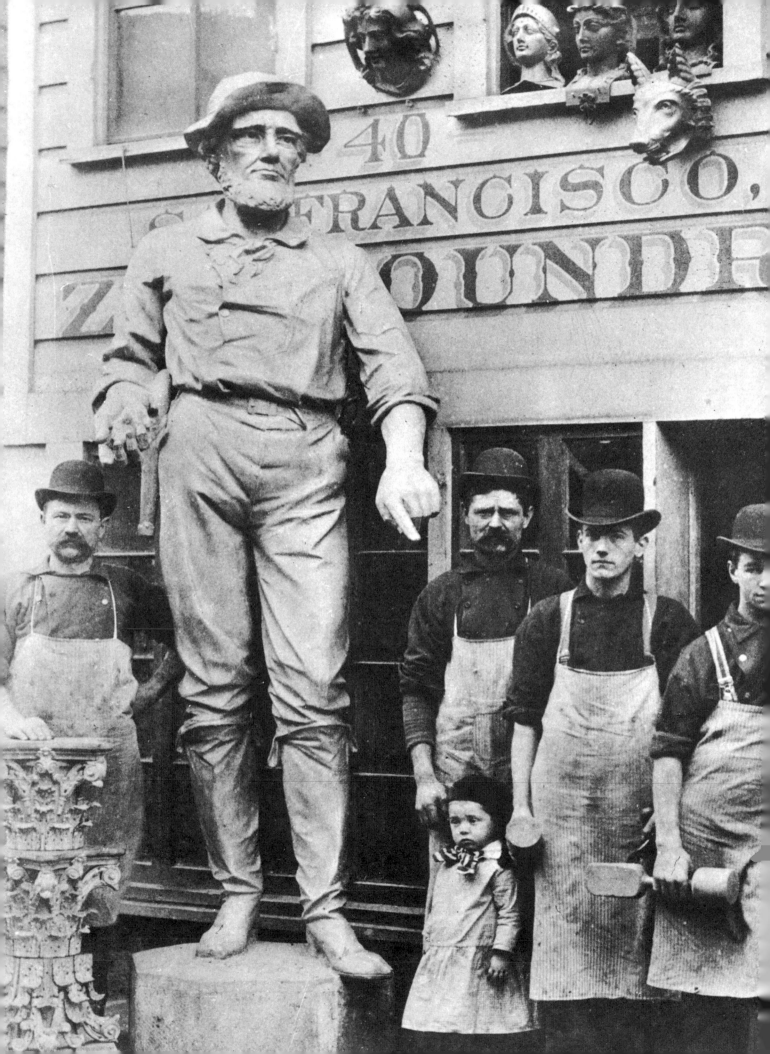

The Great Treasure Hunt

Glitter from the handful of gold that James Marshall discovered in 1848 flashed to the world. Within a few months, a torrent of young men poured into the Sierra to engage in history's greatest dig.

Goldseekers swarmed over the Sierra from east and west and fanned out over the foothills where the easy pickings lay in the river gravels. As the "color" dropped off, the miners shifted to dry gulches and sluiced them clean with man-made rivers brought in by flume. As these played out, mining operations turned to deep-rock shafts, sunk into the gold-bearing quartz, and the day of the pick-and-pan miner came to an end.

Discovery of silver in the east side of the Sierra started a second rush in the 1860s, spawning mining settlements high in the mountains, well above the snow line, some within the savage reach of winter avalanches. Bullion poured out of the high tunnels until the demonetization of silver in 1873.

The great treasure hunt opened the Sierra in more ways than one. In two decades far-ranging prospectors unwittingly discovered countless lakes, waterfalls, and streams, and revealed to the world the wonders of Yosemite and the Big Trees. The skein of trails that wandered between mining settlements and to remote mines started California's road system. Most of the hundreds of encampments that flowered, fragrant with campfire smoke and the witch-hazel scent of mountain misery, vanished; but a score of solid towns remain, some living off past glory, some serving the freeway tourist, and a tiny handful subsisting on the meager returns from gold. "Coyote holes," boarded-over mine shafts, and enormous rusting pieces of machinery, too cumbersome to steal, are scattered mementos of the fever that gripped a generation.

Foundry workers stand proudly beside the just-cast statue of James Marshall in 1890 before it was shipped to Coloma for installation on a pedestal overlooking the American River. Once in place on his lofty perch, Marshall would forevermore point down to the spot in the river where he had found the nuggets that turned the Sierra inside out.

Golden Grindstone

The first wave of gold-seekers went to work on the gravel bars in the Sierra stream beds, methodically scooping up mud and gravel and panning it for color. The noisy diggings echoed to the ring of pick and shovel, the rattle and rumble of stones in sluice boxes, the cries of muleteers cursing their stubborn charges along the trails. Within a few months, nearly every Sierra placer had been panned and the easy pickings exhausted. Miners were forced to adopt progressively more elaborate means for extracting gold from larger quantities of less and less valuable ore. As time advanced, the lone miner was displaced by teams, then by companies, and finally by corporations. (*Right*): Giant arrastra at Sierra City in 1890 was a great technological improvement over the ancient device introduced by Mexican miners in the 1850s. Run by electricity, this gawky contraption could process tons of ore. As in its burro-powered antecedents, the gold ore was ground to powder by large flat stones dragged around the circular, water-filled bed. Gold was attracted to quicksilver in solution, whence it was later extracted.

Improvised Rivers

After the miners had exhausted the sand bars in the running streams, they turned to beds of dry creeks. A few men became expert at the delicate art of sifting dry sand and blowing away all but the tiny specks of gold, but many more favored creek beds that came to life during the rainy season. Some of these diggings proved extremely profitable because the gold was coarser than that in a bed of a running stream, which ground the metal to a powder. Impatient miners, unwilling to wait for the rain-activated creeks, contrived their own streams. Rivers were dammed, as at Columbia (*right*), and water carried by flume (*above*) to the dry diggings. So popular was this device that six thousand miles of flumeways threaded the gold region by 1859. Costly to construct and maintain, flumes were vulnerable to economic fluctuations in the diggings, and many water companies went bankrupt.

Except for the bulldozer, there is probably no invention of man that did more to alter the Sierra landscape than the hydraulic monitor, which dissolved whole mountains and left scars, notably at Gold Run and Malakoff, which have not healed after a century. Invented in 1852, monitors washed millions of dollars of gold from the higher elevations before they were finally turned off by legislation that prohibited dumping mining debris in rivers that emptied into the Sacramento Valley. Thousands of acres of farmland around Marysville had become silted over, leading to scores of lawsuits that eventually shut off the streams. Basically a super fire hose, the water cannon produced a stream powerful enough to kill a man who strayed into its force. The streams ran night and day, sometimes for months, washing gravel into canal-size sluice boxes where the gold was recovered. Enormous quantities of earth had to be moved to justify such profligacy. Occasionally, a softened bank would collapse and bury monitor operators under tons of mud. Fellow operators hastily flushed them out, half drowned, with streams from other nozzles.

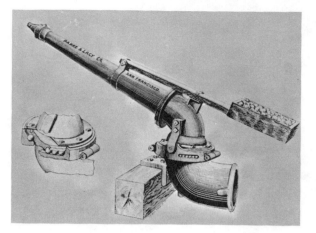

Catalogue drawing of a monitor reveals its deadly anatomy. Water, already under enormous pressure, was piped to the large intake and squeezed down to the small outlet whence it roared with fantastic force.

Washing Mountains Out to Sea

Floating Gold Mines

An endless belt of buckets scooped gravel from the river bed and dumped it on sorting tables aboard, which mechanically separated the gold-bearing sands from river rock. The latter was expelled from the side or rear.

Gold dredges arrived in the mining country almost as early as the first Argonauts of '49. The contraption above, paddling up the Sacramento River under full sail, arrived in the diggings in 1849. Like the monitor, the dredge was designed to process vast quantities of gold-bearing earth. And like the monitors, they left scars on the landscape that have not healed. As they moved slowly along a river or within a man-made lake, the dredges tossed to one side useless river rock, forming miles of levees of round stones resembling cannon balls that are still a blight along some of the rivers. Millions of these were used in building the Oroville Dam in the 1960s, but there are still a few billion left, baking in the sun.

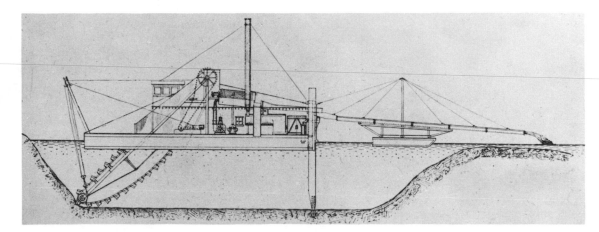

More sophisticated descendants of the clumsy model of 1849 (which did not prove out) operated profitably until devaluation of gold in the 1930s. Some were disassembled and shipped to foreign gold fields. One lone survivor somehow remained in operation until 1968.

Mile-Deep Mining

As surface deposits became exhausted, miners dug down into the heart of the mountains to reach the lodes that were thought to be the source of the free gold in the stream beds. Whole forests were felled to supply timbers for bracing mine shafts and galleries, firewood for steam plants, and charcoal for ore processing. The need to haul cumbersome mining machinery to remote claims prompted the building of hundreds of miles of mining roads, many still in use as part of the state highway system.

Deep mines required huge waterwheels, steam plants, and finally electric power to hoist men and ore, force air down into the hot workings, and run the thundering stamp mills.

Men working a mile down inside the earth were always one spark away from disaster. Worst mine tragedy in California's history occurred in 1922 deep in the Argonaut Mine at Jackson where forty-seven miners suffocated from a fire. Last message of the doomed men (*right*) was scrawled on a rock.

Cutaway of a ten-stamp mill: Ore carts rolled out of the mine tunnel (*right*), dumped their loads into hoppers that fed the rock to ponderous iron stamps, which, operating like ganged pile drivers, pulverized the rock. The powdered ore was then fed to settling tables where it was mixed with mercury and piped to vibrating tables below that shook the gold free. So much mercury was used in the gold country over the last century that game fish in Carquinez Strait today carry traces of this poisonous element, absorbed from the contaminated river water.

MINER'S HOME.

MINER SICK.

MINER'S DREAM.

MINER COOKING.

LETTERS FROM HOME.

WASHING DAY.

THE HONEST MINER'S SONGS.

The One he Sung at Home.

TUNE—*Susannah.*

Like Argos of the ancient times,
  I'll leave this modern Greece;
I'm bound to California Mines,
  To find the golden fleece.
For who would work from morn till night
  And live on hog and corn,
When one can pick up there at sight
  Enough to buy a farm?
    CHORUS.— Oh California! that's the
      land for me,
I'm going to California the gold dust for
    to see.

There from the snowy mountains side
  Comes down the golden sand,
And spreads a carpet far and wide
  O'er all the shining land;
The rivers run on golden beds,
  Oe'r rocks of golden ore,
The valleys six feet deep are said
  To hold a plenty more.
    Oh California! &c.

I'll take my wash bowl in my hand,
And thither wind my way,
  To wash the gold from out the sand
In California.
  And when I get my pocket full
In that bright land of gold,
  I'll have a rich and happy time:
Live merry till I'm old.
    Oh California! etc.

The One he Sings Here.

TUNE—*Irish Emigrant's Lament.*

I'm sitting on a big quartz rock,
  Where gold is said to grow;
I'm thinking of the merry flock,
  That I left long ago:
My fare is hard, so is my bed,
  My CLAIM is giving out,
I've worked until I'm almost dead,
  And soon I shall "peg" out.

I'm thinking of the better days,
  Before I left my home;
Before my brain with gold was crazed,
  And I began to roam.
Those were the days, no more are seen,
  When all the girls loved me!
When I did dress in linen clean,
  They washed and cooked for me.

But awful change is this to tell,
  I wash and cook myself;
I never more shall cut a swell,
  But here must dig for pelf.
I ne'er shall lie in clean white sheets,
  But in my blankets roll;
An oh! the girls I thought so sweet,
  They think me but a fool.

MINER'S SLUMBERS.

FRIENDS IN COUNTRY.

MINER'S CLAIM.

MINER'S CABIN.

FRIENDS IN CITY.

SATURDAY NIGHT.

MINER'S EVENING.

To escape the tedium of the diggings, miners turned to simple dissipations, most notably, gambling—a companionable extension of their quest for instant wealth. "Almost every store-tent had one or more rude tables where card playing was indulged in 'for the drinks,'" wrote a forty-niner, "or where monte, the favorite gambling game, was played for dust, and at night these places were alive with miners purchasing supplies or trying their luck at the tables."

The Miners' Lot

Letter sheets, such as this often reprinted sample, were bought by the thousands and sent to the folks in the States to show what life was really like in the diggings.

If the number of bitters and nostrum bottles unearthed at town dumps in the gold region are any indication, the miners were hypochondriacs to a man. For a dollar, miners could cure themselves of minor ailments, but for ten dollars, they could buy surcease from "weaknesses arising from youthful indiscretions."

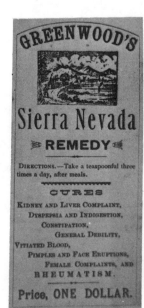

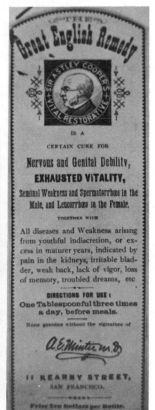

Fire!

"I'm never coming back to this place again!" shouted the angry bar owner in Truckee as he slammed the front door. To which his infuriated wife retorted, "I'll say you won't!" and she tossed a lighted lantern into a corner. The resulting fire, which consumed not only the bar but most of Truckee as well, became known as "history's most expensive family spat." Conflagration was a constant fear in the tinder towns of the gold country. Lighted and heated by open flame and protected by scanty water supplies, the settlements were plagued by fires. Conflagrations consumed Nevada City and Columbia (*right*) once, Truckee twice, and Grass Valley three times.

Volunteer fire companies attracted the towns' elite. In some settlements, youngsters formed junior fire brigades, such as this auxiliary to Sonora's Eureka Fire Engine Company in the 1870s.

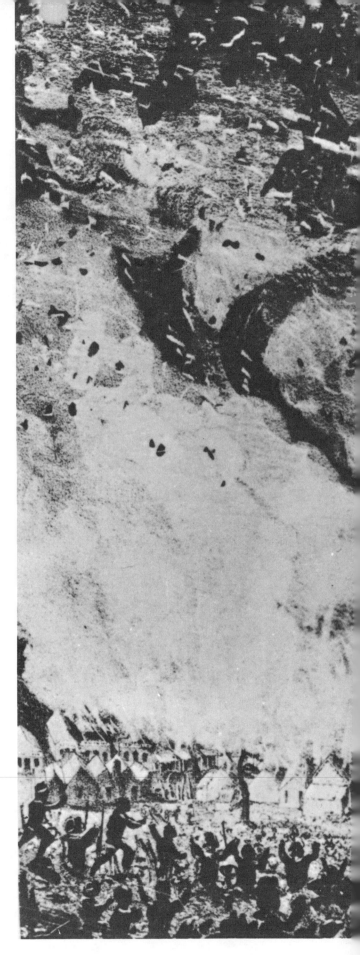

For the first few years of the gold rush, lonely young men outnumbered girls ten thousand to one, but after the rush subsided, the men who stayed sent for their womenfolk and life quickly returned to normal. Picnic excursions, such as that of this starched group from La Porte, once more became a standard Sunday feature.

The Miner Domesticated

The Fourth of July was always celebrated with gusto in the mining camps, an occasion for roistering, fireworks, and flag-wrapped speeches. As the years passed, the holiday lost none of its vigor, but took on softer features. The wagon leading this 1901 parade in Sonora carried five occupied baby carriages.

Once a miner, always a miner. Domesticated the miner may have become, but he never lost his prospector's instincts. Here, men are looking for flakes of gold exposed by rains in the middle of a street in Sonora.

Roads to Bonanza

"Far down the canyon, winding in even grade around spur after spur outlined by low clinging clouds of red dust, we could see the Great Sierra Mule Train—that industrial gulf stream flowing from California plains over into arid Nevada, carrying thither materials for life and luxury. In a fast, perpetual caravan of heavy wagons drawn by teams of 6 to 14 mules, all the supplies of many cities and villages were hauled across the Sierra at immense cost with such skill of driving and generalship of mules as the world has never seen before." So wrote Clarence King, describing a trip over the Placerville–Carson City road in 1870.

Road development in the Sierra had been given a desultory start by the gold rush. In the 1850s a fluid maze of trails and so-called roads linked the transitory mining camps, and freighters and stagecoaches visited the established towns on regular schedules. By 1857 one large stage company covered a thousand miles, with nine hundred horses and one hundred and ten coaches.

For decades, the trans-Sierra routes were in much the same condition as when the first goldseekers crossed them. Little better than game trails, the passes were impractical for vehicles and were traversed by long files of pack animals. Under pressure from the mountain counties, the California legislature passed the Great Wagon Road Act in 1854 for a trans-Sierra road, but little was done to implement it until the discovery of silver in the Comstock Lode in Nevada in 1857 started "the greatest mass movement of men, wagons, materials, animals, and bullion known to history." The road to Nevada was frantically built with pick and shovel and maintained by toll collectors who found a real bonanza in the fees they pocketed. The teeming road declined after 1868 when the railroad absorbed the traffic.

Thundering down a rutted Sierra road, a coach-and-four heads for Truckee in a swirl of dust. During the long rainless summers, Sierra roads were thick with dust that "surpassed belief." "Husbands came home after stage rides so begrimed that neither the wives of their bosoms nor the mothers who bore them could recognize them."

Mushing Through the Snow

When the snow was too deep for stages, imaginative substitutions were improvised. An expressman for Wells Fargo & Company harnessed a crossbreed of Newfoundlands and Saint Bernards to a sled capable of handling 250 pounds and a passenger, and established an express service "rewarding to himself and very beneficial to the community of Quincy. Storms were no hindrance to the enterprise, which continued for a .decade."

Snowshoes for horses! Where the drifts were not too deep, horses could plod through the snow when fitted with special iron snowshoes, eleven inches square, and held in place with turnbuckles. The savvy animals took to the footwear instinctively, and high-stepped their way without stumbling or clanging.

A warming bottle of Blue Lightning helps travelers to survive the
bone-chilling ride over the Placerville–Carson City road in 1871. Traffic
continued across this pass right through the winter, with interruptions for
periods of heavy snow. When road conditions were too treacherous for
wheeled vehicles, stage sleighs took over, and when nothing could get
through, passengers were cached in wayside inns where they hibernated for
days at a time while the blizzards howled outside. Teamsters who were rash
enough to challenge the elements suffered dire fate. Horses froze to death in
harness and the remains of more than one improvident teamster were not
recovered until spring.

Nose-to-Tail Traffic

Traffic jams have been a fixture of the Sierra passes since the 1860s when the heavy two-way flow of goods and people choked the narrow one-way roads, as in this 1865 drawing of what is now U.S. 50. Stopovers to rest the winded animals and restore the shaken passengers were frequent—in 1859, there were eighty-one inns between Placerville and Sacramento alone. On any given day, there might be three thousand teams winding over Echo Summit (then known as Johnson's Pass) and five hundred teams and a hundred and fifty men seeking overnight shelter. Crystal Lake House (*above*) was a popular stop on the Dutch Flat and Donner Lake wagon road in the 1860s. Like all but a tiny fraction of its fellows, this hostel vanished, leaving behind only a depression that marked its well-stocked cellar and mounds of broken bottles, long since picked over by collectors.

Hand-Cut Roads

Five-ton freighters crawl up the east side of the Sierra over a narrow road hand-cut through the jumbled terrain with pick, shovel, and wheelbarrows. Barely one-wagon wide, the roads had occasional turnouts where vehicles could pass. Uphill traffic had the right-of-way over downhill; loaded wagons, over empties. In case of a breakdown, rules of the road required the team immediately behind the one in trouble to help. Reward for this assistance was by custom the bells of the distressed team.

Passage of horses, wagons, and muleskinners was eased by a host of patented oils, ointments, greases, and liniments that were applicable indiscriminately to man, beast, and vehicle.

Muleskinners' Mystique

Supply wagons skirting the edge of Donner Lake in 1866 carried payloads comparable in tonnage to a modern truck-trailer combination. A sturdy mule could pull a thousand pounds and a team of twenty could thus account for a ten-ton load, usually divided between a wagon and trailer. On steep grades, the teams were doubled or the trailer left behind for later retrieval, for it was important not to force the animals to pull beyond their capacity. Once strained, the animals would never work again for anyone. On downgrades, the muleskinners struggled to keep the cumbersome wagons from running away and sweeping them and their teams to a frightful death in the bottom of a canyon. To hold back the wagons, a skinner applied brakes, locked the wheels, attached sledlike skids, or cut down a tree and chained it behind as a drag.

Teams were usually all-mule, except for the wheel position where the stronger and heavier horses were needed to handle the bouncing wagon tongue. The muleskinner controlled the team with a long jerk line, a bag of small throwing pebbles, a blacksnake whip, and torrential profanity.

Rounding a sharp turn on a narrow mountain grade called for a mule ballet that was fascinating to behold. To maintain a steady pull on the chain that pulled the wagon, mules had to step across the chain and pull from an angle as they rounded the turn, then step back into line when the turn had been completed. The brass bells on the leaders were specially made in Switzerland and tuned to a major chord. Their cheery cadence and merry jangle echoing through the still mountains reassured both the animals and the skinner.

Dedicated to Miss Lillie Swift.

FRANK MONK
Schottische

"Keep your Seat Horace, I'll get you thar on time."

Composed by

J. P. MEDER.

CARSON CITY, NEV.

PUBLISHED BY JOHN G. FOX, CARSON CITY, NEV.

"Keep Your Seat, Horace"

Most famous of the many famous stage drivers who rocketed frightened passengers over the Sierra was Hank Monk who, it was said, could turn a coach-and-six in the street at full gallop. Besides outwitting his share of bandits, delivering treasure boxes through rain and snow, Hank was elevated to national renown by Mark Twain, who described at tedious length an episode in Hank's rambunctious career when he gave a hair-raising ride over the Sierra to a presidential aspirant, Horace Greeley, in 1859. Greeley, then a prominent newspaper editor, had come west to drum up interest in the proposed Pacific Railroad. He followed the trail of the projected route across the country and met Hank Monk at Carson City, Nevada. Late for a speaking engagement in Placerville, Greeley placed his fate in the reins of Monk, and the resulting ride was described by Twain in *Roughing It* and in three hundred platform lectures. Briefly, the tale ran like this: "Hank Monk cracked the whip and started off at an awful pace. The coach bounced up and down in such a terrific way that it jolted the buttons all off of Horace's coat, and finally shot his head clean through the roof of the stage, and then he yelled at Hank Monk and begged him to go easier—said he warn't in as much of a hurry as he was awhile ago. But Hank Monk said, 'Keep your seat, Horace, and I'll get you there on time.'"

Twain did not regard this as a particularly amusing anecdote, but he swore that he had heard it 482 times "in all the multitude of tongues that Babel bequeathed to earth, and flavored with whiskey, brandy, beer, cologne, sozsodent, tobacco, garlic, onions, grasshoppers— everything that has a fragrance to it through all the long list of things that are gorged or guzzled by the sons of men." He reported, "I have seen it in print in nine different foreign languages; I have been told that it was employed in the inquisition in Rome; and I now learn with regret that it is going to be set to music."

OVERLEAF: Bright red Concord coaches with chrome yellow undercarriages offered the closest approach to deluxe travel in the Sierra for many years. Their excessive weight (1,200 pounds) kept them off the steepest grades, where the inelegant but lighter mud wagons carried the passengers and express. The heavy coach shell was slung on long leather straps, which gave a measure of pendulous comfort to the passengers but mainly eased the strain on the valuable horses. So sturdily were the Concords built that some ran for sixty years over the mountain roads, and a hundred survivors inhabit museums throughout the west today. (Painting by Gutzon Borglum, courtesy of Joslyn Art Museum, Omaha)

ARREST. STAGE ROBBER.

☞ These Circulars are for the use of Officers and Discreet Persons only. ☜

About one o'clock P. M. on the 3d of August, 1877, the down stage between Fort Ross and Russian River, was stopped by a man in disguise, who took from Wells, Fargo & Co.'s express box about $300 in coin and a check for $205 32, on Granger's Bank, San Francisco, in favor of Fisk Bros. On one of the way-bills left with the box, the robber wrote as follows:

> I've labored long and hard for bread—
> For honor and for riches—
> But on my corns too long you've trod,
> You fine haired sons of bitches.
>   BLACK BART, the Poet.

Driver, give my respects to our friend, the other driver; but I really had a notion to hang my old disguise hat on his weather eye.

Respectfully
B. B.

It is believed that he went into the Town of Guernieville about daylight next morning.

———

About three o'clock P. M., July 25th, 1878, the down stage from Quincy, Plumas Co., to Oroville, Butte Co., was stopped by one masked man, and from Wells, Fargo & Co.'s box taken $379 coin, one diamond ring said to be worth $200, and one silver watch valued at $25. In the box, when found next day, was the following: [Fac simile.]

here I lay me down to sleep
to wait the coming morrow
perhaps success perhaps defeat
And everlasting sorrow
I've labored long and hard for bread
for honor and for riches
But on my corns too long youve tred
You fine haired sons of bitches
let come what will I'll try it on
My condition cant be worse
And if theres money in that Box
Tis munny in my purse
Black Bart
the. Po8

About eight o'clock A. M. of July 30th, 1878, the down stage from La Porte to Oroville was robbed by one man, who took from express box a package of gold specimens valued at $50, silver watch No. 716,996, P. S. Bartlett, maker.

It is certain the first two of these crimes were done by the same man, and there are good reasons to believe that he did the three.

There is a liberal reward offered by the State, and Wells, Fargo & Co. for the arrest and conviction of such offenders. For particulars, see Wells, Fargo & Co.'s "Standing Reward" Posters of July 1st, 1876.

It will be seen from the above that this fellow is a character that would be remembered as a scribbler and something of a wit or wag. and would be likely to leave specimens of his handwriting on hotel registers and other public places.

If arrested, telegraph the undersigned at Sacramento. Any information thankfully received.

J. B. HUME, Special Officer Wells, Fargo & Co.

Hazards of the Open Road

Holdups, runaways, and wrecks spiced the lot of the stage traveler. Runaways were fearsome experiences for those who lived through them. Spooked by a wild animal, a falling rock, or a thunderclap, teams would sometimes take flight. On level ground, a skilled driver could turn them in a circle and let them run themselves out; but on a winding mountain grade, the driver was usually helpless, and many out-of-control stages went over the brink. Highwaymen (*left*) waylaid stages where the teams slowed down for sharp turns or steep grades. Most publicized of the Sierra bandits, Black Bart held up twenty-eight stages, often leaving behind a scrap of sassy verse, and eluded Wells Fargo detectives for eight years before he was betrayed by his laundrymark, captured, and imprisoned.

New Ways to Carry the Message

Bactrian camels, those here on their way to Nevada in the 1860s after crossing the Sierra, were originally imported by the Army for an experiment in desert transportation. The ungainly beasts fared well in the waterless wastes, but found the rock-strewn mountain trails painful going. The sharp rocks cut their tender pads, requiring the protection of leather shoes. Camels so terrified oxen, mules, horses, and tavern habitués that they were prohibited from traveling the roads or entering towns after dark in Nevada. When one caravan attempted to cross Carson Pass, angry bullwhackers and teamsters drove them back and forced them to struggle down a precipitous alternative. The moody animals were reputed to enjoy a good view and would seek a scenic vantage point in the mountains before folding up for the night. (Also see page 111.)

Communications across the Sierra became instantaneous with the completion of the transcontinental telegraph in 1861, here memorialized by the Spirit of Communication tiptoeing along the wire with a message of hope for the war-torn nation.

Conquest by Rail

In "an act of madness or inspiration" a visionary engineer and a quartet of Sacramento merchants set out in 1862 to build the western end of a transcontinental railroad through impenetrable Sierra passes and with tin-cup financing.

The young engineer behind the scheme, Theodore Judah, had come west in 1854 to help build a railroad from Sacramento to Folsom. Obsessed with the vision of a transcontinental rail line, he zealously promoted his dream with congressmen, bankers, and businessmen, finally enlisting the support of four merchants whose names have become part of the litany of California history—Leland Stanford, Collis P. Huntington, Charles Crocker, and Mark Hopkins. Together, these men formed the Central Pacific Railroad Company.

In 1862 Congress authorized construction of the line as a war measure and designated two companies to build toward each other: the Central Pacific eastward from Sacramento, the Union Pacific westward from Omaha. The problems of building a railroad over the Sierra were so formidable that the lawmakers stipulated that the two companies meet at the California border, anticipating that it would take the Central Pacific as long to lay 140 miles of track to the state line as it would the Union Pacific to put down 1,400 miles of rails from Omaha. As it turned out, a superb combination of engineering skill, managerial prowess, and the dogged labor of twelve thousand Chinese drove the Central Pacific's rails across the two, snow-covered summits of the range, through fifteen tunnels, around precipices, all the way across Nevada, and halfway through Utah before the rival tracklayers were met in 1869. As an engineering accomplishment, the rail conquest of the Sierra is justly regarded as one of the major construction feats of the nineteenth century.

Supply train backs up to the railhead at Dixie Cut in 1866, sixty-three miles and eight months' hard work beyond the start of construction. The first of the thousands of Chinese laborers are already at work, using only hand tools and one-man, one-horse dumpcarts.

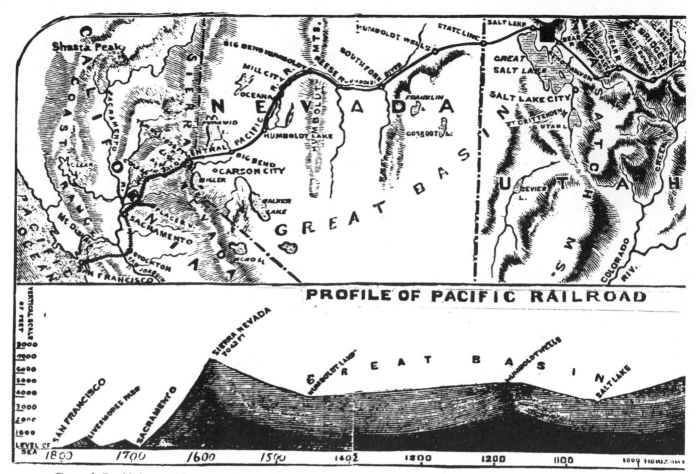

PROFILE OF PACIFIC RAILROAD

Central Pacific's tracklayers took twenty-seven months to batter a path eighty-six miles up to the summit of the Sierra and seven more to descend thirty-five miles to the state line. From there on the gangs breezed five hundred and fifty miles across the Great Basin in less than a year to meet the rival rails at Promontory (indicated by black square on the map).

Hand-Carved Right of Way

Cut-and-fill, cut-and-fill offered the only way to drive the level roadbed through the up-and-down terrain. Wagon roads could ride with the topography, but not a railroad right-of-way.

Chinese laborers, digging through a forested mountain slope, haul away the rock in carts and dump it into an eighty-foot-deep ravine to bring the roadbed up to level. Slow as it was, this process was faster and cheaper than trestle building.

The Chinese Breach California's Great Wall

Inch by inch, the Chinese laborers carved a path through the Sierra, using only pick, shovel, and cart. Years before the introduction of the pneumatic jackhammer, this work had to be done by hand and required thousands of men. Cuts were made in several levels, permitting simultaneous deployment of several teams of men.

Tea carrier, standing outside a tunnel entrance, kept crews supplied with lukewarm tea, a dietary preference that saved the Chinese from the ailments that afflicted Caucasians who drank the often polluted mountain water.

Logistics of Supply

A blur of activity, the main street of Cisco was jammed with freight wagons in 1867–68 while it served as the advance supply base for the ten thousand men and one thousand horses working on the line. From here, a steady parade of cumbersome, two-ton freighters hauled supplies to the crews blasting their way across the summit or headed up the Dutch Flat and Donner Lake wagon road to the forward construction forces working on the other side of the Sierra. At the start of the colossal undertaking, half a century before construction of the Panama Canal, every rail, spike, bolt, nut, fishplate, locomotive, and boxcar had to be brought around Cape Horn, often in peril of capture by Confederate frigates. An armada of chartered vessels eluded the patrols and landed tons of equipment in San Francisco. The supplies were shipped up the Sacramento River, loaded on trains, then transshipped by wagon. The freighters carried a mixed bag: firewood, ties, hay, water, hand tools, hardware, kegs of blasting powder. For the Chinese: dried oysters, abalone, cuttlefish, bamboo sprouts, mushrooms, Chinese bacon, peanut oil, and tins of tea.

Even locomotives were hauled to the job site. In 1867 an engine was sledged over the Sierra in winter for use on the tracks being laid to the east while work was suspended on the summit tunnels because of deep snow. Wrestling the twenty-ton dead weight over the crest was a man-killing struggle, but not as terrifying as the descent, where the monster threatened to snap its snubbings and crash down the mountainside.

NEW EXPRESS GALOP

"Cape Horn" Placer Co, Cal, and View of the Sierra Nevada, on the Line of the Pacific Rail road.

Copy righted.

As the Central Pacific inched its way into the High Sierra, the company ran excursion trains to spectacular overlooks as the work advanced, hoping to gain popular and political favor. Here, in 1866, excursionists are viewing the American River from Green Bluffs, seventy-one miles from Sacramento.

"Take Your Seats for New York"

By 1868 trains were crossing the Sierra and a year later, transcontinental runs were in daily operation. Exclamation point in every trans-Sierra trip was a stop at "Cape Horn," a rocky eminence named with grudging respect by workmen who had had difficulty blasting a path around it. Famous for its view, it was honored in 1870 with a song (*left*), dedicated to the "lady patrons," who, according to Lucius Beebe, were "a negligible quantity—and largely weren't ladies, either."

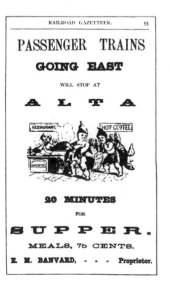

The dining car did not become a fixture of the transcontinental trains until 1890. Previously, trains stopped briefly at mealtime so passengers could bolt down food, as this 1870 advertisement indicates.

81

Snowfall far in excess of original estimates piled up to twenty feet in 1867, smothering tracks, bunkhouses, roads and halting construction. To clear the tracks, bucker plows, pushed by as many as fifteen locomotives, rammed a path through the deep drifts. The work was slow and often hazardous. Snow slides sometimes toppled plows off the rails. Blinding blizzards or a thick blanket of snow could conceal sunken rails, open switches, or ice slicks that could derail a plow.

Enemy in White

After the track had been cleared by the plow, armies of shovelers had to dig away the banks. During the severe winter of 1889–90, four thousand shovelers worked to keep the line open.

Efficient snow dispersal had to await the invention of the rotary plow, introduced about 1890. Its spinning blades could eat up in an hour the distance that had previously taken a whole day. This type of plow is still the basic snow-fighting machine on the Sierra crest.

Railroading in a Barn

The disastrous winter of 1867 proved that snowplows alone could not keep the high passes open and that additional protection from the crushing mass of snow would have to be improvised or construction would be seriously delayed and the projected Pacific Railroad might find itself a summer-only operation. The solution: roof over the tracks and the construction zones where the snow drifted deepest or was most likely to avalanche down on the right-of-way. Begun in 1868, thirty-seven miles of shed were completed by 1869, consuming in the process whole forests along the way—sixty-five million board feet.

Staunch construction was mandatory to keep the sheds from collapsing under the thousands of tons of snow that covered them.

The snowsheds proved their worth from the start and a few miles are still a visible feature of the Sierra landscape. Some of the first sheds were damaged by slides, and for many years the structures were plagued by locomotive-started fires; but the wrecked portions were redesigned and a water train was developed to douse fires and drench the sheds during dry months. To keep passengers from developing claustrophobia while riding through the long wooden tunnel, openings were left at intervals so travelers could enjoy a stroboscopic view of the Sierra.

Snowbound
Streamliner

Driving into the teeth of a hundred-mile-an-hour blizzard in January 1953, the Southern Pacific's streamliner "City of San Francisco" crept slowly down Donner Pass even though at full throttle, and ground to a halt near Yuba Gap, stuck in twenty-foot snowdrifts. The 226 passengers and crewmen aboard were excited by the adventure at first, but after three days of icy imprisonment few were smiling, and some recalled with foreboding the tragic fate of the Donner Party in the pass below a little more than a century earlier. Massive rescue efforts were promptly started by the railroad, supplemented by help from highway and utility crews and the Army and Navy, but attempts to free the pinioned train were crippled by the unceasing storm. A rotary overturned, killing its engineer, and rescue trains stalled en route. Sole hope for release rested with a single highway plow, eight miles down the road, which had already been overworked. Because of the relentless fury of the blizzard, the highway crew took three days to reach the trapped streamliner. By then, conditions aboard the train were turning critical. Supplies of food and medicine were running low .and the steam heat was about to run out. Rescuers reached the train on the third day, which dawned clear but piercingly cold, and led the passengers to the plowed highway, their faces protected from the stinging chill by pillowcases with eyeholes cut into them. The frozen train was pulled free by giant tractors.

The winter of 1952–53 was one of the half dozen remembered in California history and folklore for their severity. It ranks with the terrible season of 1846–47 that trapped the Donner Party, that of 1889–90 that nearly shut down the trans-Sierra railroad, the 1937–38 season that piled sixty-seven feet of snow at Norden, and the notable snowfall of 1968–69.

Could this entrapment happen again? A repeat performance is doubtful. Since the 1950s the railroad has acquired more powerful snowplows and locomotives with twice the horsepower and has installed an array of electronic warning devices that preclude a train's being caught in a similar predicament.

Second Rail Crossing

Forty years passed before a second railroad ventured across the Sierra. In November 1909, the Western Pacific completed its line through the boulder-choked Feather River Canyon, a route earlier considered by the Central Pacific but rejected as too difficult to traverse. The first passenger train to Quincy was welcomed in 1910 by Arthur Keddie, the WP's one-man equivalent of the CP's Theodore Judah and the Big Four. For the sixty-eight-year-old engineer, this dramatic moment marked the fulfillment of a lifelong dream, and he was overcome with emotion.

Flag-waving children, dressed in their Sunday best, turned out at every stop for the jubilant welcoming of the first WP passenger train over the Sierra.

"The great heart of the state throbs at the triumphal entry," proclaimed a newspaper of the welcoming of the first train to the railhead in Oakland by an immense and exuberant crowd. In further celebration, a four-mile-long parade marched up Broadway.

Laying track in 1906–9 was a very different operation from the backbreaking task that had faced the CP's section gangs in the 1860s. Improvements in grading equipment enabled the railroad to build through a canyon that had been too formidable for the technology of the CP's day. Pneumatic drills, jackhammers, and powerful new explosives made it possible for the WP to carve a niche through the rocky defile, and special track-laying trains, such as this one, substituted mechanical aids for manpower and muscle.

End of an Era*

In celebration of Western Pacific's "Ruby Jubilee," November 1, 1949, three historic trains meet at Spanish Bridge in the Feather River Canyon. On hand, the Central Pacific's famous "Jupiter," co-star of the wedding of the rails at Promontory, Utah, in 1869; Western Pacific's "Engine No. 94," which had pulled the first passenger train through the canyon forty years before; and the shiny new streamliner "California Zephyr," then initiating vista-dome service to the East. Little did the promoters of this ceremony suspect that within twenty-one years all three of these trains would be museum pieces. A victim of airline competition, the last "Zephyr" carried a load of doleful railroad buffs on March 21, 1970, thus ending its notable record for fine service to the traveling public.

The magnificent scenery of the Feather River Canyon, visible from glass-domed cars, provided the principal lure in Western Pacific's advertising. But even this enticement could not keep the trains filled and the operation became unprofitable. Before its discontinuance, the "Zephyr" was averaging so few passengers that they were sometimes outnumbered by the crew.

OVER THE HIGH SIERRA AND THROUGH THE COLORFUL COLORADO ROCKIES!

TWO-DAY SCENIC RAIL CRUISE

ABOARD THE VISTA-DOME California Zephyr

No matter what train you take to Chicago, the fare is equally low. But only the **California Zephyr**, the most talked-about train in the country, gives you these

EXCLUSIVE EXTRAS!

Scheduled for sightseeing! Exciting, daytime, see-level views of America's most magnificent scenery . . . the Feather River Canyon, California's Sierra Nevada, and the Colorado Rockies.

Unique San Francisco Cable Car Room buffet lounge serving beverages and inexpensive meals. De-

luxe Dining Car and Observation Lounge Car, too.

Not one but five roof-top Vista-Domes, glass-enclosed penthouses with 120 unsold, unreserved extra seats where you can look up, look down, look all around.

The Zephyrette—your hostess— comments on scenic highlights, makes Dining Car reservations in advance, helps make your trip even more interesting and enjoyable.

No extra charge for reserved, reclining seats with leg and foot rests. *(All types of Pullman accommodations also available.)*

DAILY FROM SAN FRANCISCO TO CHICAGO
VIA SALT LAKE CITY AND DENVER
ONLY $67.50 (FAMILY FARES EVEN LOWER!)

Make your reservations early. (This is "the most talked-about train in the country"!) See your travel agent or your nearest Western Pacific Ticket Office.

James J. Hickey, Director of Passenger Sales, Western Pacific, 526 Mission St., San Francisco

Please send me complete information about the California Zephyr.

Name _____

Address _____

City _____ State _____

WESTERN PACIFIC

Incomparable Yosemite

Yosemite was one of the earliest of California's alpine spectacles to reveal itself. Once its sublime features became known in the 1850s, the valley began to attract pilgrims as soon as the first trails were opened and the unfriendly Indians neutralized. Travel was further stimulated by a freshet of magazine articles, newspaper accounts, books, photographs, and museum exhibits of heroic paintings as large as drawing-room rugs.

To many who came to see if it "lived up to the brag," the scenic revelation was a catalyst for further exploration in quest of other Yosemite-like canyons. But to most of the millions who have been drawn to the valley, the cliffs and waterfalls are sufficient unto themselves, "glorious beyond the highest anticipation."

Located at the mid-point of the range, Yosemite is in a meaningful sense the heart of the Sierra. It is the gateway to the northern and southern Sierra, a bridge between the tawny foothills and acerbic High Country. It was here that the concept of a National Park system was first hammered out. Yosemite was John Muir's headquarters, the first mountain home for the Sierra Club, the first park in the country to be set aside for purely scenic value, and in 1890 it became the nation's third National Park. Its sculptured landscape has served as a workshop and training school for map makers, geologists, engineers, and conservationists who have applied the lessons studied here to the national scene.

In 1855, forty-two cast-iron tourists endured the arduous descent into the valley. In 1970, 2,300,000 converged on the park, most of them sardined in the narrow valley. The day is not far off when tourists will have to secure individual admissions to this all-too-popular park.

First known sketch of Yosemite, this theatrical interpretation of Yosemite Falls was drawn in 1855 by Thomas A. Ayres, a devotee of the Hudson River School of painting. It was one of a series published the next year that helped focus world-wide attention on the wonders of Yosemite.

Destination for the Durable

First tourists to visit Yosemite were of a durable stripe. The only way to reach the valley for twenty-three years after its discovery by the white man was by an interminable horseback ride over Indian trails. Stagecoach roads soon reduced the number of saddle-sore miles, but until 1874 travelers still had to endure the final descent on the backs of "sorry brutes, who looked at us with eyes of sullen reproach." The giddy scramble down the cliffs of the Merced Canyon terrified "even the bravest, who leaned timorously toward the mountain side and away from the cliff, ready for a spring."

Resorts blossomed early. The first ones (1856) were built of hand-sawn timber, partitioned with cotton cloth, and stocked with furniture carried over the trails on muleback. The sumptuous Sentinel Hotel (1876–1938) was one of several first-class resorts that appeared in the valley. Actually a cluster of hotels near the river, the Sentinel was torn down in 1938 by the Civilian Conservation Corps. Only remnant is Sentinel Bridge. Resort hotels were also built on the tip of Glacier Point (1872–1969) and between Vernal and Nevada Falls (1870–90) in the Little Yosemite area.

Discovery
of Yosemite

The first white man to look down into the great chasm of the Merced is generally conceded to be the trapper-explorer Joseph Reddeford Walker, who led a mounted party of fifty trappers along the north rim of the valley on their way to Mexican California in 1833. Although proof of Walker's discovery has been debated for a century by historians, Walker had no doubts: his tombstone in Martinez bears the inscription "Camped at Yosemite, Nov. 13, 1833." Walker's party returned east via a low-level pass that now bears his name.

First white men to set foot in the valley was a punitive expedition known as the Mariposa Battalion that entered the valley (*right*) in pursuit of marauding Indians in 1851. The militia returned empty-handed but open-mouthed about the spectacular scene they had stumbled upon. The elusive Indians soon returned to the attack in a desperate attempt to drive the white men away from their tribal lands. A second expedition relentlessly pursued, captured, and expelled the tribe to a reservation near Fresno. The Indians were presently allowed to return to Yosemite on pledge of peaceful intention, but in a last outbreak of violence, a party of braves murdered two prospectors (*left*) camping in the valley and provoked forceful retaliation.

These trees "of a noble lineage that bridges humanity back through eons to the age of reptiles" were brought under governmental protection from logging in 1864 with the creation of the Yosemite Grant by Act of Congress.

The First State Park

First state park in the country, the Yosemite State Grant was confined to the valley and to Mariposa Grove, thirty-five miles to the south. Setting the stage for the development of the national park system, the grant represented the first time a legislative body had sequestered federal property because of its scenic values. In 1890 the National Park was created to protect the watershed of the famous valley. For fifteen years, Yosemite was administered by both state and federal officials, before the state finally returned the inner park to the larger one. Initial boundaries of the National Park included more territory than is now encompassed by the park.

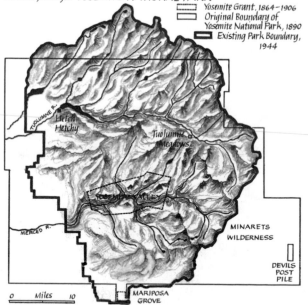

Boundary Changes YOSEMITE NATIONAL PARK

Yosemite Grant, 1864–1906
Original Boundary of Yosemite National Park, 1890
Existing Park Boundary, 1944

Unwitting founders of Yosemite
National Park, thousands of sheep
grazed in the Sierra meadows and
clipped off the ground cover that
protected the watershed. With nothing
to slow it down, rain water sluiced
the stripped meadows (*right*) into the
valleys below, causing floods and
silting of streams. To prevent this
destruction, John Muir and others
campaigned to expand the borders of
Yosemite so sheepmen would be
banned from using the fragile
meadows. Even after the park was
legislated, shepherds trespassed for
decades, convinced that they had prior
rights to the high country.

The Tourists Come Rolling in

Two eras of transportation: After 1874, stagecoaches rolled down the
switchbacks of Big Oak Flat road into the valley. The coaches stopped briefly
at Oh My! Point to allow the passengers to gasp at the first view of the
valley, then started down the zigzag. Stagecoaching was no picnic excursion.
When the passengers were not choking in dust that sometimes concealed from
view the driver, horses, and even fenceposts along the road, they were
battered and tossed by the rocky highway and terrified by the precipices a few
inches beyond the skittering wheels. Horse-drawn stages monopolized Yosemite
traffic for forty years until 1907, when a railroad was completed from Merced
to El Portal, where travelers transferred to tallyhos and later (1915) to buses.
That the rail route was a popular choice can be guessed from the mountain of
baggage (*above*) awaiting transfer to the valley. In its turn, the railroad was
gradually pushed aside by competition from the motor car, and finally put
out of business by a disastrous flood in 1937 that washed out miles of rails
and roadbed and destroyed bridges. Tracks were taken up in 1945.

OVERLEAF: Of the many artists who painted Yosemite scenes, few
were more idolized than German-trained Thomas Hill (1829–
1908) who created a number of huge, dramatic canvases such as
this one now at the Crocker Art Gallery, Sacramento.

Bear-feeding sideshow drew tourists to the garbage pit where dozens of black bears rummaged through the smoldering refuse, defending their chosen heaps against all challengers, unfazed by exploding containers and bursts of flame. Fascinating to tourists but rough on bears, the circus was discontinued in 1941.

Old Favorites: Bears and Embers

This is no joke. Bruin is probably less interested in learning the mileage to Tenaya Lake than he is in demolishing the sign. For unfathomed reasons, bears destroyed so many wooden trail signs that steel ones had to be erected in their place. Rangers, trying to plumb the bears' psychosis, tested different colors, paint formulas, and kinds of wood, but the bears impartially clawed apart all the variants that were offered them.

"Let the fire fall!" bellowed a voice in the hushed silence of Camp Curry and down into the night a streamer of sparks cascaded from Glacier Point, sometimes accompanied by the quavery singing of "Indian Love Call" from the open-air stage at Curry. For ninety-six years, off and on, this nightly spectacle enchanted visitors after its introduction in 1872 by the proprietor of the Mountain House on the top of Glacier Point. Initially, the ceremony was performed with oil-soaked gunny sacks tossed flaming over the brim, sometimes enlivened with a stick of dynamite. Over the years, other diversions have been proposed: colored searchlights, fireworks, and, more recently, flashing neon. The firefall was discontinued in 1968 by the Park Service.

On the tip of Glacier Point, the firemaster listened for the faint but clearly audible call from the valley 3,250 feet below, then launched into his dervish dance, pushing a quarter cord of fir bark embers over the brink with a long-handled hoe.

Yosemite vs the Motor Car

(*Above*) One of the first cars in Yosemite (1900), a Stanley Steamer. (*Left*) A Studebaker perched on the Overhanging Rock in 1910 for a publicity stunt.

The first "blunt-nosed mechanical beetles to puff their way into the park and mingle their gas-breath with the breath of the pines and waterfalls" (Muir) arrived in 1900, duly alarming park authorities who promptly banned them because they frightened horses and endangered stagecoach passengers. When motor cars were finally permitted to enter in 1913 they did so under a code of sixty-five restrictions, such as: no smoking in the car, a six-mile-an-hour speed limit, a honk at every turn, and five minutes to disembark passengers. Violators of the rules were subject to "ejectment without remission" of their $5.00 fee. With the opening of the Coulterville Road to automobiles in 1913, followed the next year by the Wawona and Big Oak Flat roads, and, finally, by the All-Year Highway from Merced in 1926, the rush of cars commenced. In the pre-smog 1920s, there were portents of the future (*above*) in the packed parking lots and holiday delays at the check-in station (*right*).

King of the Conifers

"Surely, this must be some curiously delusive dream!" mused the bear hunter when he stumbled upon a grove of mammoth trees near Murphys in 1852. When he later tried to describe the unnerving discovery to his hunting companions, they laughed at him, "supposing he was trying to perpetrate upon them some first-of-April joke." By a ruse, he lured his friends back to the grove, where "doubt was changed into certainty, and unbelief into amazement; as, speechless with profound awe, their admiring gaze was riveted upon these forest giants."

This sighting, as reported by James Hutchings, was not the first time the Big Trees had been seen by white men, but it was the first to bring the immense trees to the attention of the world. "But a short season was allowed to elapse before the trumpet-tongued press proclaimed the wonder; and worshippers flocked to the Big Trees to see for themselves the astounding marvels about which they had heard so much."

Not only did people come to the trees—some of the Big Trees were brought to the people. Towering sequoias were dismantled in the forest and reassembled to amaze gaping crowds in eastern and European cities. Back in the forest, the carcasses of the exported giants were converted into tourist curiosities.

Discovery of these "noblest of a noble race" precipitated a tug-of-war over an appropriate botanical name. British botanists wanted to name the tree for the Duke of Wellington, "the greatest of modern heroes." Americans opted for George Washington, but the name *Sequoia gigantea* was finally chosen because of the tree's similarity to the Coast Redwood, already named for Sequoya, renowned leader of the Cherokees. The two redwoods are now known to be separate species and the Big Tree carries the unwieldy name *Sequoiadendron giganteum.*

Painting a portrait of the Wawona Tree and its giant companions in 1901, artist Chris Jorgensen fulfills an urge that has beset three generations of painters, poets, musicians, and photographers to memorialize the giant trees in art.

Mammoth Grove

So great was the interest in the Big Trees, following their discovery in 1852, that a resort was built in 1853 at Calaveras Grove, the site of the Discovery Tree. Located on one of the main Sierra passes (Ebbetts), the grove was accessible alike to curiosity seekers and muleskinners—even to a camel caravan shown plodding through the trees, en route to the mines of Nevada in 1861. The resort burned down in 1946 and the area is now a state park.

The Discovery Tree was felled in 1853 and its huge stump smoothed off for use as a dance floor. Nearly twenty-five feet in diameter, it supported a cotillion in 1872 of thirty-two dancers and musicians. The stump was later roofed over and made into a pavilion, which served as a dance hall, newspaper office, and exhibit room. The stump minus its gazebo is still a popular attraction in the Calaveras Grove. Visitors stand transfixed in the center of the great circle, mesmerized by the colossal scale of the tree.

Undaunted by the enormous size of the Discovery Tree, a crew of five toppled it after twenty-two days' work in 1853. They drilled a multitude of holes through the bole and sawed the wood between. Though completely severed, the tree stood defiantly, then blew over with a seismic crash while the men were at dinner.

Since the introduction of the box Brownie, tourists have been striking antic poses in, on, around, or under these giant trees, recording for family and friends the momentous encounter and somehow identifying mystically with these oldest of living things.

Little People and Big Trees

First drawings of the Big Trees in the 1850s were delightfully inaccurate, often sketched by artists who had not had the good fortune to see these "mountains of wood." The great trees were first thought to be cedars.

Cheerful visitor to Calaveras Grove peers squirrel-like from a giant knothole in a fallen sequoia.

Sequoias on Tour

The Mark Twain Tree: Felled for science in 1891 at age 1,341 years, this tree was cut so two slabs from its trunk could be sent to museums, one to the American Museum of Natural History in New York, the other to the British Museum. Riggers worked with block and tackle in installing the cumbersome slab in New York. Once in place, it was smoothed, polished, and banded; it is still on display. Too bulky to ship east intact, the nine-ton slab was split into twelve handier segments by pounding wedges into the grain. The huge slice was cut twelve feet above the ground and measured sixteen and a half feet in diameter inside the bark. The stump is still standing in Sequoia National Park. A fifteen-cent brochure pointed out that this tree was a sapling at the end of the Roman Empire, when Europe was being overrun by the Goths, Vandals, and Franks.

Flyer promoting another reconstituted Big Tree, large enough to "store" 117 standing men, drew gawkers to an exhibit in New York in the 1850s. Visitors were offered a chance to sign a register so their "grateful" children could see who of their fathers had visited it.

World's Fair Tree

Official exhibit of the U. S. Government at the Chicago World's Fair in 1893 was a hollowed-out, thirty-five-foot section of a Big Tree, cut in Kings Canyon. Because scoffers had challenged the authenticity of previous reconstituted sequoias, this one was cut with a floor between its two stories that was formed of a disc of the trunk itself. Sawyers link hands (*above*) around the base of the General Noble, the immense tree they are about to cut down under government contract. When it fell (*below*), it took the scaffolding with it and nearly killed the loggers, who jumped onto the stump as the thousand-ton tree groaned and toppled. With no handholds, the four men spread-eagled on the tall stump, which vibrated for twenty minutes, nearly flinging them off. The stump was all that was wanted for the exhibit—the rest of the giant trunk was split up for stakes—and it was hollowed out and carefully cut into staves that could be reassembled to form a two-story "house." *Above right,* the loggers are cutting the upper story, forming it of seventeen-foot staves. Pierced back together, the stump appeared in the fair and then was moved to the Mall near the Smithsonian Institution in Washington, where it served as a gardener's shack until it mysteriously disappeared in the 1930s when the Army took over the area where it had stood.

Wawona Tree
31 *B.C.*–*A.D.* *1969*

Equal to the Grand Canyon and Old Faithful as a symbol of the National Parks, the Wawona Tree in Yosemite attracted several million pilgrims from all over the world to pass through its tunneled base in the eighty-eight years of its life as a tourist attraction.

The tree was originally tunneled out in 1881 by five brothers who were paid $75 to cut an opening large enough to admit a loaded stagecoach. Immediately tourists began to come to the Mariposa Grove for the unique experience of driving through a tree. Other tunnel trees were chopped out, one not far from the Wawona Tree itself, and another in the Tuolumne Grove, but the practice was stopped by the National Park Service when it took over the park in 1890.

Most photographed tree in the world, the Wawona Tree was a "must" stop for every camera-laden visitor. Kings, Prime Ministers, and five Presidents had their photographs taken emerging from the tunnel. Here a troop of World War I cavalry, guns at the ready, pose for the inevitable photograph.

"Your money or your life!" A "highwayman" stops a stagecoach with a menacing "loaded" champagne bottle in an early gag shot.

Death of a colossus: Heavy snows in the raging winter of 1969 finally toppled the 234-foot giant in its two-thousandth year. The enormous tree was found to be rotted. Messages of condolence—telegrams, poems, letters, cards—poured in to the park from all over the world.

Utopian Loggers

Working with hand tools and wheelbarrows, utopian socialists labored for four years to build a steep mountain road to the groves of Big Trees that they claimed under timber patents to twelve thousand acres. The men were members of a unique co-operative, the Kaweah Colony, formed in 1884 to establish a base for world-wide socialism in the mountains near present Sequoia National Park. The plan was to log off the trees and mill them into lumber, which would be sold on the open market to earn funds for starting a socialist state. The five hundred-member group adhered to the then-novel doctrines of the eight-hour day, forty-hour week, and equal pay for women. Creation of Sequoia National Park in 1890 blocked the colony from further logging and the group disintegrated soon afterward, riven by internal friction.

End of the road. National Park gate, built across the colonists' road, effectively barred access to the Big Trees. This road, with an eight-mile extension, later became the main vehicular access to the park.

No. 108. SERIES "C." **100,000 MINUTES.**

THIS BILL OR TIME-CHECK is issued and put forth by

THE KAWEAH CO-OPERATIVE COLONY COMPANY, LIMITED, A JOINT STOCK COMPANY,

Of KAWEAH, Tulare Co., Cal., in return for services rendered by a Member of said Company, and is evidence that said Member, or his successor, the BEARER, if he also is a member, has performed for said Company the number of MINUTES' labor set out above, in payment for which he has agreed to receive in return either an equivalent amount in time of any other labor the Company may be able to render, or goods at cost which the Company may have on sale at said time, or credits upon membership fee or share subscription under regulations provided by the Membership and Trustees.

Irrespective of this certificate the Dividends issued yearly on the hours worked are payable to the credit of the member who did the work and not to the holder of this certificate. This certificate is void in the hands of a non-member of the Company and is NOT TRANSFERABLE to persons outside of said Company.

Issue of July 1, 1889.——DISCOUNTING PROHIBITED. GOOD ONLY BETWEEN MEMBERS.——

100,000 Minutes = $500. *Wm Christie* Treasurer. *J Martin* Secretary.

Members were paid in time-checks instead of money, negotiable only in the colony store. A two hundred-minute check was worth a dollar; a twenty-five-minute check was good for a meal. A medallion was issued for twenty-four hours' work.

OVERLEAF: Charming watercolor of the Fallen Giant in Calaveras Grove by artist Constance Gordon-Cumming in 1878 dramatizes the size of the downed tree but accurately depicts the ragged, shallow root system that anchors these elegantly balanced monsters. (Courtesy of the Oakland Museum)

Sequoia Gigantea.
Calaveras.
California.

C. F. Gordon Cumming
July 30.
1878.

Father of the Forest.
Estimated height. 450 feet.

Timber Harvesting

For thirty years beginning in the 1850s the lumber needs of the booming young state were so insatiable that it is a wonder any timber trees are now standing in the Sierra.

In this frantic interlude, scores of mining towns and miles of flumeway were hammered together in the foothills. Across the Sierra crest, wood-burning locomotives pulled trains over millions of ties cut along the right-of-way, across uncounted wooden trestles, and through forty miles of timbered snowsheds. To the east in Nevada, the Comstock mining boom swallowed whole forests into the ground to shore up mine shafts and galleries and consumed cordwood by the trainload to fuel steam-powered machinery. While down in the Central Valley, clapboard farming communities sprang up as the railroad opened up the agricultural lands.

The felling and processing of Sierra lumber called forth daring improvisations in excess of those usually expected of the loggers' dangerous and ingenious trade. In the roadless timber belt, the steep gorges, high mountains, and boulder-strewn rivers forced solutions to everyday logging problems that would have delighted Paul Bunyan.

Even the two-thousand-year old sequoias were not immune to the axe and the saw. A single Big Tree was equal to five sugar pines in volume and could yield three thousand fence posts—enough to support a wire fence around eight thousand acres—plus enough shingles to roof seventy or eighty cottages. The Monarch of the Forest was a lumberman's dream.

Unbridled logging practices eventually brought about governmental regulation—but not before two thousand acres of Big Trees and the forests around Lake Tahoe had been stripped bare. The introduction of forest management practices in 1914 has helped to stabilize the industry and bring balanced use of the forest preserve.

Pushed off balance by wedges pounded into a saw cut halfway through its trunk, a ponderous Big Tree falls to a thunderous death in a bed of soft branches, specially prepared to cushion the impact. The stirring spectacle is an old story to the spectators who watch nonchalantly, seemingly unperturbed.

Prideful Paul Bunyans

Felling the gargantuan trees was a formidable task and the loggers and their families proudly posed with their conquered giants for itinerant photographers. Favorite Sunday poses: a girl astride a horse is the fall cut of a Big Tree or an assemblage of wives, families, girl friends, dogs, and horses festooned over the trunk of a downed monarch.

So large were the sequoia slabs that often the only way to split them was with a charge of black powder, which, more often than not, blasted the wood into unmanageable chunks.

As indicated in this 1901 photograph, sequoias outside the National Park boundaries were being felled long after the bulk of the Sierra groves had been brought under federal protection, beginning in 1890. A small amount of sequoia logging is still going on today.

Take Every Tree

Stripping every tree from the forest was the goal in the early days of logging the Sierra. Legislative controls were slow in being enacted because of an overwhelming demand for lumber to build a mushrooming state, a conflict in jurisdiction between government agencies entrusted with control over logging practice, and general confusion about property rights in the mountains.

Unrestrained logging created severe erosional damage in some areas when the forest cover was removed and nearly eliminated some species of trees. The eight thousand sequoias cut down in Converse Basin in the 1890s will not be replaced before the year A.D. 4000—if then. Often, loggers left a strip of trees as a screen along highways so the public would not be distressed by the carnage. Forest preserves were finally established in 1903 and four million acres brought under governmental control. Forest management practices introduced in 1914 have helped to stabilize the logging industry and bring balanced development of forest resources to the Sierra. However, the demand for lumber is insatiable, and even today, lobbyists are pressing for a return to the old method of stripping all the timber trees from the forests.

Greased Lightning

Once felled, the downed tree was stripped of its limbs, sometimes its bark, and the naked trunk was then sawed into standard lengths for the sawmill, which was often several miles away.

The long journey from the site of the cutting to the final destiny with the screaming band saws brought forth ingenious methods for transporting the heavy, dead-weight logs over terrain that was too steep, rocky, or gullied for roads. Dry chutes, formed of paired logs laid side by side for miles, offered a simple and economical channel for sliding logs to the mill. Smoking from friction of rubbing against the greased track, a giant log screeches down a dry chute (*above*), heading for a rendezvous at the mill.

Saw logs trailing rocket
tails of smoke and flame
thundered down the
chutes at express-train
speed and plunged into
Lake Tahoe, exploding the
water into geysers of spray.

Venerable predecessor of
the dry chutes, skid roads
formed of cross ties
threaded the timber lands.
At a leisurely pace, oxen
pulled log trains over the
cross ties, which were
sloshed with animal fat
(forty gallons to a mile)
by a tallow boy.

Winch, Cable, and Steam

Vertiginous cable incline from El Portal (*left*) brought logs down from the forested upland 3,500 feet above the settlement, where they were transshipped by rail to the mill fifty-five miles down the line. Two flatcars were linked together by cable. Weight of the loaded one descending pulled the empty car back to the crest. The operation ran from 1912 to the 1940s. A similar line once rose from the shore of Lake Tahoe (1880–90), bringing logs down the mountainside and dumping them into the lake where they were rafted to mills on the shore. Long gone, this installation is remembered only for a place name—Incline—and the deep scar it left on the mountain, still visible ninety years later.

Sierra rivers, unlike those in other timberlands, were mostly unfit for log transport. Of uncertain flow in summer, the time of heaviest logging, boulder-choked, or too short, the streams were of little use to loggers. One exception: tons of cordwood were sent boiling and leaping down the steep rivers on the east side to feed the fireboxes of mine, locomotive, and lake steamer boilers in the 1880s.

Faithful donkey engine, surrounded with its crew and a snaggle of cable, was a muscular addition to any logging crew. Supremely self-sufficient, it could pull itself to any location by reeling in cable fastened to a distant tree, and its boiler lived off the scraps of the logging operation. By reeling in cable, it could topple trees, snake logs out of the woods, pull loaded flatcars up inclines. Donks were treated with respect—and fear. Boilers were known to explode, and the cables were terrifying lashes of destruction when they broke under tension.

Mills in the Woods

Logs were sorted by size, grade, and type of wood at collecting points in the woods. Here, a string of random cut is being hauled in on the dry chute (*right*) and matched logs are being readied for a tow to the mill on horse-drawn trams. Pulling log trains was a dangerous trade for horses —the unfortunate animals were sometimes overtaken on downgrades by the cumbersome log trains and crushed to death.

Mills were built close to the logging area to shorten the distance for trundling the saw logs from the cut-over land. This extensive layout once operated in Converse Basin—within the boundaries of present-day Sequoia National Park. Finished lumber was whisked by flume sixty-five miles down the mountains to Sanger in the San Joaquin Valley for stockpiling.

Man-Made Rivers

An innovation in lumber transportation, the V-shaped flume revolutionized
the logging industry after its introduction on the eastern Sierra in 1859. The
tortuous topography and unraftable rivers of the Sierra initially confined lumber
delivery to the immediate neighborhood of the mills. Flumes provided a swift
and direct connection with lumberyards in the Central Valley and in time
permitted the Sierra lumber to compete with that shipped in from Oregon and
the north coast of California.

The man-made streams provided more than lumber transport. Simple boats
—shaped like hog troughs—carried mail, messages, provisions, trout and venison
packed in snow, and even people. Invalids and accident victims, sometimes
accompanied by relatives or doctors, were flumed down to the lowlands for
medical care. In the southern Sierra, loggers sometimes rode down the flume
for a night on the town and returned the following day via horse and buggy.
A machine was developed by one inventor that would crawl back up the
flume, using the structure as a wooden railroad, but it was never built.

Though invaluable and capable of transporting hundreds of thousands of
board feet of timber, flumes were wasteful. Boards had to be cut extra length
to compensate for the battering they took in transit and many were lost in
accidents.

Flume tenders, stationed at turns or sections where the water
slowed down, prodded reluctant boards on their way, broke up
jams, and fished out damaged lumber. Other tenders patrolled
the flumes, walking along spray-drenched catwalks, sometimes
hundreds of feet above the ground.

When a flume failed, the damage could be a near disaster, as this 1888 scene suggests. Workmen repairing a break on another flume near Tahoe were unexpectedly showered with trout that had become trapped in the inlet and carried to the break. (*Below*): This intricate trestle was 110 feet high, cost $160,000.

"A Perilous Ride"

Most famous flume ride in the Sierra involved two lumber tycoons and a reporter whom they dared to accompany them down a twenty-three-mile descent in 1875. "The terror of that ride can never be blotted from the memory," wrote the newsman. "A flume has no element of safety. You cannot go fast or slow at pleasure; you are wholly at the mercy of the water. I was really scared almost out of reason. Every object I placed my eyes on was gone before I could clearly see what it was. Mountains passed like visions and shadows. It was with difficulty that I could get my breath . . . We made the entire distance in less time than a railroad train would ordinarily make, and a portion of the time we went faster than a railroad train ever went. We were a wet lot when we reached the terminus." One participant estimated their speed at a mile a minute, another guessed their top speed at one hundred miles an hour! Afterwards the shaken reporter went on his way, but the two millionaires took to their beds.

More powerful and less temperamental than oxen or mules, cumbersome steam-powered tractors took over the task of hauling lumber in some areas of the Sierra.

Steam Lumber Transport

Hundreds of crooked miles of steel were laboriously laid in the Sierra between 1890 and 1914 for shortlines to haul logs, lumber, marble, mine products, talc, cattle, and tourists. These railroads snaked their way through the pines over roadbeds "full of switchbacks, swaybacks, humpbacks, trestles, torrents, and terror."

"Take your best girl and come along. Music going and coming." Excursions over logging railroads drew capacity crowds in the early 1900s. Here, a party stops for the inevitable photograph on the way to a Sunday baseball game at Angels Camp in 1900.

Prideful roundhouse workers at Groveland (1922) encrust a hundred-ton workhorse belonging to the Hetch Hetchy Railroad (1914–1949), a sixty-eight-mile line built to carry cement to the construction site of O'Shaughnessy Dam. This cog-driven locomotive was typical of the doughty engines—saluted as the "Artillery of Commerce" by a Mother Lode orator—that chugged over the shortlines. It was relatively light in weight, extremely powerful with traction to every wheel, and flexible enough with its three trucks to "round three sides of a schoolhouse" without derailing. The luxuriant cowcatcher was no mere ornament on locomotives that had to run the gauntlet through open range where cattle "became twice as valuable when struck by a train as they were on the hoof."

The "Artillery of Commerce"

Diminutive predecessor to the monster on the left, seven-ton "Betsy", the first locomotive in the pine woods, worked for the Madera Pine Co. in the 1880s.

Cracked skulls, broken bones, scalds, and knife wounds were normal occupational hazards for miners, lumberjacks, and railroad section hands. Small hospitals were maintained by the larger logging camps and every large town had a dispensary and an overworked doctor—especially burdened on weekends when fortified railroad gangs brawled with teamsters and cowhands. The injured were sometimes whisked to bigger hospitals in railroad ambulances, such as this flange-wheeled hybrid, which also carried off the victims of the all-too-frequent train wrecks.

Sierra Stewardship

The guardian angel of the Sierra, John Muir, relaxes with a book alongside a trail in Kings Canyon. Though only one of a succession of zealous conservationists dedicated to preserving the Sierra from exploitation, Muir influenced a wide following through his writings, lectures, and personal contacts.

"Nature's sublime wonderlands, however well guarded, have always been subject to attack by despoiling gain-seekers and mischief-makers of every degree from Satan to Senators, eagerly trying to make everything immediately and selfishly commercial." So scolded John Muir in 1908 in an attack on a plan to dam Hetch Hetchy Valley. The sermon came directly from his battle-scarred heart, for he had already spent some years on the firing line with other conservationists fending off the forays of "despoiling gain-seekers."

When California became a state in 1850, the forty million acres of the Sierra belonged to the federal government. Use of the land was limited by rules that applied to flat farming country and nothing in the regulations governed logging, grazing, or despoilation of scenic wonders in the mountainous preserves. Into this inviting vacuum, loggers, sheepmen, and resort developers happily stepped. By 1860 hundreds of thousands of sheep were cropping the watershed ground cover, trees were dropping by the mountainside, and canvas inns were springing up alongside two-thousand-year-old trees, three-thousand-foot waterfalls.

Efforts to save the state's dwindling natural heritage were started in the 1860s by a handful of enlightened, dedicated, and adroit conservationists, soon joined by the eloquent young Scot, John Muir. The struggle was unending—it is still going on—but with persuasion and guile, the conservers won some major victories for the public good, and lost a few disheartening battles. In the front rank, the Sierra Club in 1892 took over the job of bolstering the conservation agencies and keeping vigilant guard over the public's fragile Sierra heritage.

Mapping the Unmappable

In the 1860s, the bristling High Sierra was terra incognita to all but a few sheepherders, cattlemen, and hog drivers who grazed their animals in the high meadows. The first map makers had to break their own trails through the granite wilderness and to innovate techniques for charting the jumbled mass of peaks and chasms that lay before their instruments. Distances were figured by triangulation between pinpoints of light, flashed by mirrors packed to the summits of distant peaks. An eight-inch mirror could reflect the sun's rays 120 miles through the clear Sierra air.

Intrepid members of the field party sent to map the southern Sierra in 1864—James T. Gardiner, Dick Cotter, William Brewer, and Clarence King —braved snowstorms, freezing nights, rain, deep chasms, and "unscalable" peaks, and brought back the first scientific report on the unknown High Sierra, stimulating mountaineers to conquer the challenging land.

This vast wall of mountains rising beyond a tremendous canyon is what met the eyes of the 1864 surveyors after they had climbed what they had innocently thought to be the crest of the Sierra. Instead of a view of Owens Valley and the leagues of the desert beyond, they faced a second range some 1,500 feet higher than the 13,000-foot peak on which they stood. They reluctantly concluded that "to cross this gorge and ascend the eastern wall of peaks was utterly impossible." But such a challenge was more than one member of the party, Clarence King, could resist, and he and James Gardiner clambered through the almost impassable labyrinth in five days, in one of the major mountaineering conquests of the Sierra history.

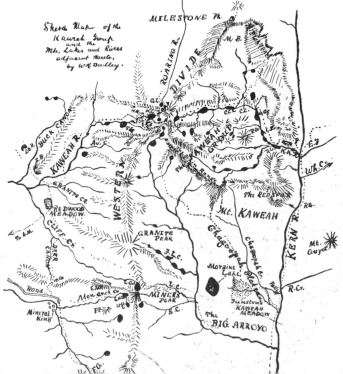

The Sierra Club co-ordinated the mapping of the Sierra from 1893 until the U. S. Geological Survey took over the task. Maps such as this one appeared at intervals in the *Sierra Club Bulletin.*

Conquest of the Summits

Charles F. Hoffmann on the summit of Mount Hoffmann, 1867. Renowned for his cartographic skills, this young German engineer set high standards for the mapping of the Sierra during his four-year assignment with the California Geological Survey. His meticulous map making influenced cartography in America for decades.

Judge E. C. Winchell on the summit of Mount Winchell, 1868. Reflecting the exhilaration felt by the first explorers of the High Sierra, Winchell was photographed at the climactic moment when he named a 13,749-foot peak for his cousin, a distinguished geologist. Wrapped patriotically in the flag and bolstered by a "test sample" from a wicker-woven flask, he "addressed formal salutations to the witnessing mountains and fired double-charges of gunpowder over the canyon and forest, arousing crashing reverberations that leaped from cliff to distant cliff, swiftly redoubling in the morning air." The exuberant Winchell was just one of the many mountaineers who flocked to the high country after publication of the official reports by the Geological Survey in the late 1860s.

Two women mountaineers stand triumphantly on the tip of a pinnacle in
Gardiner Basin in 1896. Women were not far behind the so-called stronger sex
in the exploration of this wild up and down land near Mount Whitney.

Muir the naturalist: Bonneted Sierra Club hikers listen in rapt attention as Muir, in his seventies, points out some secret of nature to them. An ecologist before the word was even invented, Muir's interests ranged over a wide spectrum, and he early reported on the interrelationship of plants and animals, mountains, and men. His theories on the glacial sculpturing of the Sierra, conceived from field observation, were initially derided but are now generally accepted.

Muir the Student: Young John, age twenty-three at the time he entered the University of Wisconsin, was noted for his brilliance and for his peculiar genius as an inventor, expressed in hand-carved clockwork contrivances. Even as a college freshman, he sported the beard that was a lifelong trademark.

John o' the Mountains

Self-styled "poetico-trampo-geologist-bot, and ornith-natural, etc.!" John Muir devoted most of his adult life to the study and preservation of the Sierra. He arrived in Yosemite in 1868 at age thirty and over the next twenty years he explored every nook and peak, sketching and making notes. Nothing missed his alert interest, from a floret to a forest fire. He believed that nature in its wilder forms reflected God and refreshed man, and he published his glowing observations in articles and books that still delight lovers of the Sierra. In mid-career he shifted his attention from nature study to the defense of the beleaguered Sierra and became a militant conservationist.

Muir the Conservationist: The gentle naturalist turned rabid conservator in the 1870s after he became convinced that unbridled exploitation of the Sierra resources by sheepmen, loggers, miners, politicians, and resort owners would destroy the usefulness of the mountains to the general public. He campaigned for National Park status for Yosemite and Sequoia, helped found the Sierra Club, convinced Theodore Roosevelt among others of the need for broadening federal protection of forest preserves, and suffered a final, crushing defeat in a battle to save Hetch Hetchy Valley from the dam builders.

Sequoia—
National Park
No. 2

The thunder of falling sequoias, cut for grape stakes, fence posts, and shingles, had echoed over more than two thousand acres before alarmed conservationists were able to halt the devastation. A crusading newspaper editor in Visalia, with the covert help of the Southern Pacific Railroad, persuaded Congress to create two National Parks—Sequoia and General Grant—in 1890 that brought the trees under permanent protection. Sequoia was formed around a grove that had been homesteaded in 1858 by a shepherd named Hale Tharp, who built a snug home in a fallen giant trunk, a novel shelter that is still on view today.

Giant of the giants, the General Sherman Tree was patriotically named in 1879 for the Civil War hero, renamed the Karl Marx Tree in 1885 by the Kaweah Colonists (see page 121), and re-named General Sherman in 1890. Ranked as the world's largest tree, it is 272.4 feet tall and 101.6 feet around at the base. Lumberman's measure: 600,120 board feet.

Twenty-Nine Year Bivouac

The parsimonious Congress that created the National Parks in California provided no funds for administration, assuming incorrectly that income from concessions would pay operating costs. In desperation, the Interior Department arranged with the Army to administer the parks —an improvisation that endured for twenty-nine years. Cavalry units patrolled the parks throughout the summer, retired for the winter. Their main task was evicting sheepherders and their hundreds of thousands of woolly companions.

Acting Superintendent of Sequoia National Park in 1903, Captain Charles Young, the third Negro to graduate from West Point, made a notable record during his assignment to the park with the 9th Cavalry, a spit-and-polish outfit known as the Black Battalion. During their stay, the troops completed the road to Giant Forest Grove that is still used as the main gateway to the Big Trees. Before Sequoia, Young had served with the Rough Riders in Cuba and had helped rescue impetuous Teddy Roosevelt in his hard-fought charge up San Juan Hill. Later, he rose to the rank of colonel and served as military attaché to the American embassies in Haiti and Liberia.

Camp A. E. Wood, 1891–1906, in Yosemite. Now the Wawona Campground.

The Muscular Sierra Club

The Sierra Club was born in a fighting mood. Incorporated in 1892 for the immediate purpose of helping defend three fledgling National Parks from interests bent on dissolving them, the club pledged itself at the start to the preservation of the Sierra. Its roster included a dedicated group of mountaineers, scientists, and zealous laymen who worked hard and devotedly to save and protect the Sierra and to promote wide enjoyment and understanding of the mountains. John Muir served as its president until his death in 1914.

Hungry members of the second annual outing line up for chow (*right*) July 4, 1902 at Kings Canyon. Outings were started in 1901 to educate people in the values of preserving mountain regions. The first parties of one hundred or more were quartered in large encampments; but later groups were scaled down in size and increased in mobility. Over the years, there are few corners of the Sierra that have not been explored by club safaris. The club now sponsors a hundred wilderness outings a year, plus an equal number conducted by its branch chapters.

LeConte Memorial Lodge, built in Yosemite in 1903, was the club's first on-the-spot base for educational programs.

"Public Welcome" reads the sign on the Lincolnesque shelter for Soda Springs in Tuolumne Meadows, acquired in 1912. The mineral springs were purchased from private owners to prevent their being exploited to the detriment of Yosemite National Park. Tuolumne Meadows has since become an important base for High Sierra activities.

The John Muir Trail

In a jubilant mood, a mounted party of Park Service and Sierra Club officials on the top of Mount Whitney celebrates the completion of the last leg of the 212-mile John Muir Trail in 1938, climaxing two decades of dedicated trail building. The dream of a north–south trail along the spine of Sierra enticed mountaineers from 1893 when the first explorations were carried out by venturesome individuals. Construction of the trail was authorized by the legislature in 1915 and stretches were built over twenty summers before it was finally completed. It is the main footpath through the high country, and from it dozens of major and minor trails radiate.

RED SLATE
MTN.

SILVER PASS
10,900'

MT. ABBOTT

MT. HILGARD 13,351'

L. THOMAS A.
EDISON
7,600'

SELDEN
PASS
10,870'

MT. DARWIN

MT. SPENCER

MT.
HUXLEY

MIDDLE
PALISADE
14,049'

SPLIT MTN.

PALISADE
CREST

MT.
PINCHOT

MT.
CEDRIC
WRIGHT

DUSY BASIN
11,300'

MATHER
PASS
12,050'

TWIN LAKES

UNIVERSITY PK.

MT. WILLIAMSON 14,384'

MT. TYNDALL 14,025'

MT. WHITNEY
14,496'

MT. BRADLEY

MT. KEITH

JUNCTION PK.

MUIR PASS
12,059'

EVOLUTION L.
10,850'

MT.
GODDARD

PINCHOT
PASS 12,050'

ARROW
PK.

MT.
CLARENCE
KING

RAE LAKES
10,550'

GLEN PASS
11,900'

BEAR CR.

MONO CR.

SOUTH FORK SAN JOAQUIN R.

EVOLUTION CR.

FLORENCE L.
7,900'

MIDDLE FORK KINGS R.

SOUTH FORK KINGS R.

BUBBS CR.

MT. BREWER

FORESTER
PASS
13,200'

TYNDALL CR.

Trail Crest

HITCHCOCK
LAKES

Crabtree
Meadow
10,500'

KERN R.

GREAT WESTERN DIVIDE

N

KINGS CANYON
NATIONAL
PARK

SIERRA NATIONAL FOREST

SEQUOIA
NATIONAL PARK

Lost Hetch Hetchy

A few miles north of Yosemite's Merced Canyon lies a parallel chasm, the Grand Canyon of the Tuolumne, a magnificent river gorge almost equal in grandeur to the more famous one to the south. As these photographs taken in 1892 and 1895 indicate, the canyon was a memorable idyl, with tumbling waterfalls almost as spectacular as those in the Merced Canyon. Camping parties packed into it (*below*) beginning in the nineties. In the early 1900s the city of San Francisco, seeking a long-range supply of water, selected Hetch Hetchy Valley within the Tuolumne Canyon as a site for a reservoir. Conservationists formed a battle line. Thundered John Muir: "Dam Hetch Hetchy! As well dam for watertanks the people's cathedrals and churches!"

Protectionists contended that the Department of the Interior had no legal right to give away a chunk of a National Park for the private benefit of a city; that there were equally desirable reservoir sites outside the Yosemite boundaries; and that the beautiful meadow would some day be needed for public recreation. The conservationists lost all three rounds. Enabling legislation was passed in 1913 and construction of the dam begun in 1915. Loss of this prolonged battle was a sobering lesson in practical politics for the Sierra Club.

Dam Builders Have Their Day

Whatever the propriety of the Hetch Hetchy decision, the actual building of the dam itself was a stunning sample of the concert of engineering know-how that major construction in the Sierra always seems to stimulate. The challenge was to build a series of dams, powerhouses, tunnels, aqueducts, and penstocks in a granite wilderness accessible only by trail, all of it remote from supply centers. The massive problems were solved with aplomb over a span of eight years, starting in 1915 with the first test drills. At the time of its completion in 1923, O'Shaughnessy Dam was acclaimed as the largest single structure on the entire West Coast. Construction was speeded by first-time use of electric power for drilling and hoisting and by a sixty-eight-mile railroad, built specially for year-round, round-the-clock hauling of cement and supplies to the site.

'THE INYO REGISTER' AND 'THE OWENS VALLEY HERALD'

(Established 1885)

W. A. CHALFANT, Editor and Owner

(Established 1908)

HARRY A. GLASSCOCK, Editor and Owner

SUPPLEMENT NUMBER ONE

Volume 1.

BISHOP, INYO COUNTY, CALIFORNIA, JANUARY 7, 1925.

No. 1.

GREED OF CITY RUINS THE OWENS VALLEY

STATE-WIDE INTEREST RISES OVER OWENS VALLEY FIGHT

What is Going on in Owens Valley Affects Every Irrigation District in California and the Laws must Define Conflicting Rights

Western history is full of "The Fight at the Water Hole."

From the first day our argonaut forefathers entered the deserts of Nevada, Oregon, and the Southwest with their covered wagons, they have had to fight for the water with which to irrigate their farms.

No community in California has been free from long litigation and few sanguinary conflicts over the right to use the water from the eternal hills.

In fact all history is filled with water fights. Concentration of all wealth and power in great cities, impoverishment and neglect of the cultivators of the soil, removal of their irrigating water by great cities, ruined Mesopotamia, Egypt, Rome, and, coming closer to modern times, France, Russia and Turkey.

And in our turn California is today rent with dissension over the rights to the waters that flow down in the streams of the Sierra Nevadas. Every irrigation district in California is fortifying itself against the encroachment of the great cities along the sea shore. State and county, city and irrigation district officials are alike disturbed over the age old question of the measure of the right to use water for domestic and for irrigation purposes.

Where is the economic line to be drawn that will define the limits to which a big city may reach in its quest for domestic water supply, and to which the cultivators of the soil that provide the food supply for those cities may extend their farms?

Is it economic to remove from any farming community the water it has developed for irrigation, for the use of a city hundreds of miles away?

Though so may be strictly legal, is there any moral right to turn back to desert a farming community that a city may thrive and grow by reason of its ability to advertise itself as owning an abundant water supply?

Is there a defect in the basic law of California in that it fails to provide for a situation such as has arisen all over the state and is now accentuated in the controversy between Owens Valley and the city of Los Angeles?

This controversy is no different to that which must be waged by every farming community, every irrigation district along the entire Sierra Nevadas, from Susanon to San Diego. Everywhere the farmers and water owners are watching with breathless interest the fight Owens Valley is making to secure justice from the city of Los Angeles.

Removal of water from such communities is like burning down a house.

While there may be every legal right to so remove the water—to burn the house, is not also compensation to be paid to the man whose water has been taken, whose house has been burned?

Does it suffice to say, "We will take no more," or "we will burn your house no more?" When the water is gone, the farm is ruined. When the fire is out the home is uninhabitable. How shall the farmer subsist and how shall the house owner find shelter?

Does it comfort him, or compensate him, to tell him that the city is within its legal rights?

"The greatest good to the greatest number" is an apt phrase.

So is "life, liberty and the pursuit of happiness."

So also is "no citizen shall be deprived of his property without due process of law."

The Owens Valley fight with the city of Los Angeles has become an acute and state-wide affair. It concerns every farmer, every banker, every merchant and every workman in California and concerns him deeply.

As always in such conflicts, personal animosities and inconsiderate, hasty action and ill-tempered pronouncements cloud the issue.

Though the Owens Valley farmers, who feel they have justice on their side, have frequently offered to submit their cause to arbitration, they have thus far made no headway against the city officials who have the matter of the Los Angeles water supply in hand.

Delay in settlement, refusal of Los Angeles to consider the moral issues involved, has alarmed every water and land owner in every irrigation district in the state of California. He is watching eagerly every move made by either side to the controversy.

The Governor of California has been drawn into the dispute. His properly equipped officials are making an exhaustive study of the matter. The Owens Valley-Los Angeles conflict has delayed practically every municipal and irrigation water project in California.

Investors in irrigation district securities are hesitating about the sale of irrigation district bonds. Guaranteed by the state of California, the bonds have heretofore been gilt-edged—are now. But there is arising a doubt of the ability of irrigation districts to resist the encroachments of the great cities that need water for domestic use.

Petty officials must be retired to their pettiness, deprived of power to cloud fundamental issues, whether they be city men, or county men.

Solution of the Owens-Valley-Los Angeles controversy must be sought and completed along lines that will establish precedent and usage for all time.

Some power must be invoked to compel attention to the moral right in the dispute between a city and a farming community.

There are certain human rights that cannot be successfully invaded by any element, however powerful.

Some Moses must come forth to define the limits of these conflicting interests. Men cannot stand with a rifle over a water hole forever!

California must not be hampered any longer by disputed water rights.

MUST HAVE PUMPING RIGHTS

From the Hill, Lippincott, Sonderregger report to the Department of Public Service, August 14, 1924.

"If it is assumed that the city acquire pumping rights in the Bishop Region and establish pumps with a maximum capacity of 150 second feet and an equal pumping development in the Independence Region, it would then be possible to pump 391,000 acre feet of water from these two underground reservoirs during the nine-year critical period without a serious lowering of the water level." (Page 12, Par. 3.)

"The acquisition of paramount pumping rights in the Bishop and Independence Regions is indispensable to an adequate development of the Owens Valley water supply." (Page 13, Par. 2.)

One of the most valuable ranches in the valley lies just north of Bishop and belongs to one family that has been in the valley over forty years. This property is made up of two or three smaller parcels that have been put together into one very valuable and highly cultivated ranch, where blooded stock is raised. This ranch

SHE FACES LIFE ALONE; MATE GONE

This woman's husband, the father of this little family, broke under the strain of the valley's water troubles, facing ruin for himself and associates, committed suicide last August. These children are the third generation of Inyo folks and their mother faces life alone.

High Price Talk Is False And No Evidence Appears For Statement to Contrary

One of the favorite statements of those in Los Angeles opposed to any attempt to bring about a settlement of the Owens Valley controversy is that land owners in Los Angeles are trying to force the city to buy their lands and water rights at a big price, trying to "hold up the city," or lands bought for speculative purposes.

The facts are these:

Of the four large holdings in the Owens Valley Irrigation district, amounting to about 6000 acres in all, one tract was inherited by the present owners and the other three were bought years ago when an assured water supply seemed a permanent condition.

The last purchase was made in 1917 by a man whose son had specialized at the University of California in agriculture and animal husbandry. This young man was employed after graduation by one of the large ranch owners of the valley as superintendent. So impressed was he with the future possibilities of Owens Valley at that time that he induced his father to buy a large ranch in the valley, to buy an abundant water supply and later to buy a cattle range, and began raising cattle for the market. Since the city began to buy water and land around him, he has abandoned, as fast as good business would allow, the ranching and cattle business and the place has been offered for sale in a communication direct to the public service commission, the value to be left to a board of three appraisers. No holdup there.

One of the most valuable ranches in the valley lies just north of Bishop and belongs to one family that has been in the valley over forty years.

is the family home and owners like these do not want to sell to the city. Like the other land owners they have signed an agreement to leave the value to a board of appraisers if the city finds it necessary to buy the property.

Another owned by a Los Angeles lawyer was bought many years ago by the present owner who fondly hoped that some day he might retire from practice and live the life of a gentleman farmer. His property is admirably suited to the creation of a country estate; but he, like the other land owners, has reconciled himself to parting with this property and like the others has agreed to arbitration of the value of this property.

The fourth large ranch is owned by a Los Angeles capitalist who loves the outdoors and wanted to create a home for his old age in the Owens Valley. He leases the property "now" and has joined with the other land owners in an agreement to sell at a price to be fixed by a board of appraisers.

Other acreage owned by the sons and daughters of the men and women who conquered the desert, watered it and established their homes in early days are now farmed by these men. In nearly every case these are the lands most hurt and depreciated by the operations of the city. A whole family of sons and daughters in one district near Big Pine were forced to sell, and one of the saddest days of last year was that on which two of these young men signed the deeds with tears in their eyes.

Men and women do not willingly give up the homes where their children were born, and money cannot pay for some strains on the heart strings. To be charged with trying to "hold up the city" hurts these people and the men who make such charges know that it hurts them—they make them for that reason, it helps break down the others.

Press of Nation Is Filled With Owens Valley Story; Their Fight Is Well Known

By HARRY GLASSCOCK
Editor Owens Valley Herald

The Owens Valley-Los Angeles water controversy has assumed a national importance as is evidenced by the courteous account of matter that was carried by the different papers of the nation during the recent trouble in Owens Valley.

The leading Eastern papers carried the story as a feature on the front page, with big scare headlines, and magazines such as the Literary Digest gave it much space. In practically all of the papers that handled the matter editorially the sentiment seemed strong in favor of the people of Owens Valley. Most of the papers deplored any lawlessness on the part of the people of that section, but still there was always a thought running through the articles that the people of Owens Valley were morally justified in the course they had taken.

This publicity has hurt Los Angeles, and hurt it terribly. There can be no question about it, for one well knows that a story is liable to grow as it travels, and truth is not always the paramount idea in modern journalism. But be that as it may, there is one outstanding feature in the entire matter, and that is that there has been some terrible wrong done to the people of Owens Valley or else such a law-abiding American community could not be stirred up to the point where they would take the law into their own hands. And this point seems to be conceded by all of the papers of the country. They may have called the men who guarded the headgates of the valley's aqueduct and allowed the city's water supply to go to waste for four days a "mob," but in many cases it was referred to in the same manner as the Boston Tea Party, and was heralded on the grounds that it was the only weapon that a defenseless people had against a strong municipality to bring their wrongs to the attention of the world. While few papers tried to justify any lawlessness that there might have been, still as far as condemning it—they did not do so in very strong terms.

Probably no city ever built on the country was built on a foundation of good will as Los Angeles has been. In every way, every day, for years past, the name of Los Angeles has been heralded to the country as standing for everything that is best—as an ideal place to live, with beautiful surroundings and a moral atmosphere that is of the highest. This word was broadcasted throughout the Eastern and Middle Western States with the result that people came here by the hundreds of thousands to make their homes in this God-favored country. Los Angeles grew like a mushroom from a small pueblo to the largest city in Western America, and this growth was made possible by the good name that Los Angeles had throughout the country — and Owens Valley water.

Now this publicity work on the part of the people of Los Angeles was a constructive work, and as such should not be destroyed. The name of this city should continue to stand for all that is right and just, for much hard work has been done to lay the firm foundation for such a name. And the destruction of this good name should be avoided, because, as we stated before, it is the very foundation of the wonderful growth of this city.

In this day and age of the world there is no reason why such trouble as there now is between Owens Valley and Los Angeles should not be settled peacefully and fairly and in a constructive way, instead of tearing down that which has been built up by hard work. There is no reason why the city of Los Angeles should be heralded to the world as the oppressor of a small community. For this is not constructive and Los Angeles, with her billions of dollars of invested capital, cannot afford to have a stigma attached to her name for fair dealing. There is too much at stake. And the cost is too great.

Business conditions in Los Angeles today are not flourishing. That is a plain statement of truth, although it is not a pleasant situation to look in the face. If you doubt it just ask your corner merchant, ask your landlord, or ask any business man. He will tell you that it is so. You may not care to believe it, is dull. That may be caused by several different things, but one thing is a certainty, and that is that the undesirable publicity that Los Angeles has had in the past by reason or account of the Owens Valley water supply has not helped any to stabilize conditions here.

People here are justified in believing

LOSS OF BUSINESS AND PRESTIGE HAS COME TO CITY'S VERY DOORS

Shortage of Water; Shortage of Power, Useless and Damaging Result of Official Double Dealing

We, the citizens of Owens Valley, believe that we have a common interest with the people of Los Angeles and the State of California.

We believe that the methods employed by your leaders and agents, to which the people of Los Angeles are indirectly party, are actually bringing more ruin, destruction and business depression upon the City of Los Angeles than are being brought to Owens Valley, deep and serious as that is.

The same warning given by Oliver Goldsmith to the people of England many years ago applies to the conditions existing in Southern California today:

"Ill fares the land, to hastening ills a prey,
Where wealth accumulates, and men decay.
Princes and Lords may flourish, or may fade,
A breath can make them, as a breath has made.
But a bold peasantry, their country's pride,
When once destroyed, can never be supplied."

We, a community of six thousand souls, actual producers of the necessities of life, without which cities cannot exist, have been pictured as a lawless element, a reckless mob. On the contrary we are a home loving people who only ask to live and let live. How could we be otherwise when we are descended from the very best blood of the pioneers who have helped to make the great state of California.

You know that a little more than a year ago Los Angeles was enjoying an era of prosperity heretofore unknown, business was moving with a feverish haste, apartment houses and office buildings could not be constructed fast enough to meet the ever-growing demand. A little later business men of Los Angeles, realizing the importance of giving permanent employment to the rapidly growing population, organized a large corporation for the purpose of fostering and encouraging factories to come to this great city.

About this time, the president of the American Manufacturers' Association, Mr. John Edgerton, visited Los Angeles and was banqueted by the Chamber of Commerce. In his wonderful address delivered on that occasion he spoke encouragingly of Los Angeles becoming a great manufacturing and export city.

In the midst of prosperity and plans for future development what happened to your city? You were notified of a great water and power shortage, you were told to reduce the light in your homes, the streets were partially lighted, street car service was greatly hampered, manufacturing and industry was crippled. How could you expect Eastern capital to come to your city, where thousands of men were being thrown out of employment, with insufficient water and power to take care of your own requirements? Thousands of people at this time were leaving Los Angeles and were spreading and exaggerating the news of your bad conditions throughout America.

As there are no coal mines in this section, Los Angeles is dependent on water and electric energy for its very existence. You were being struck in the most vulnerable point possible. The pneumonic plague and the bubonic and smallpox plague and the foot and mouth disease, which your health department stamped out in their infancy, were the least of your troubles. Epidemics come and go in every locality; but it is left to far-sighted, thinking men, to provide water, power and light for the existence of a city.

Did you know that during this great calamity, when your community was being strangled for water, millions of water was daily flowing through the irrigation canals of the Owens Valley ranches to have doubled the flow of the Owens Valley aqueduct? Did you know that at this very period the water from these great canals could have been diverted into your aqueduct and that power plants belonging to the city, which had been idle, could have been placed again in operation, all at a very nominal cost? The general loss to the city has already amounted to more than twenty times the equitable amount of compensation for this water.

We would like for a delegation of citizens, property owners and merchants of Los Angeles, in the interest of your people, to visit Owens Valley and judge for themselves. We would welcome at this time, when great water and power projects are before congress, a delegation from congress and the public lands committee, on a visit to this section, as your Owens Valley aqueduct, practically three hundred miles long, passes through government property. Other vital power propositions in which you are already interested and will soon be more vitally interested, are matters for the entire nation to consider.

When you first view Owens Valley and are personally informed, you will naturally wonder why, with these facts in possession of officials of the city, something has not already been done to relieve your immediate needs. The whole panorama will speak for itself and it will naturally occur to you that there must be some reason or motive, for not securing this water

(Continued on Page Four)

Bishop Union High School, cost $250,000, one of the best equipped high schools west of Salt Lake.

One of the deserted school houses of Owens Valley. No families live in this district now because all the farms have been bought by the City of Los Angeles, and coyotes howl now where the voices of happy youngsters once made this little school house an influence in the community for good.

Owens' Bitter Waters

On the other side of the Sierra, another contested water project made the Hetch Hetchy vendetta seem pale and genteel. The city of Los Angeles reached into Owens Valley in 1907 to draw much-needed water from Owens Lake, filled by east-flowing Sierra rivers, and residents of the valley suddenly found themselves forced off their lands and out of their homes. The twenty years of controversy that followed were clouded by suicides, dynamitings, vigilante raids, sabotage, and, tragically, embezzlement by the leader of the valley rebels. Inexorably, Los Angeles got its water; but traces of the vitriol expressed in the newspaper at the left persist today in some sections of the valley. *Above:* concrete diversion weir at the head of the aqueduct; *right:* pipe sections for one of the great syphons.

Summer in the Highlands

"Camp out among the grass and gentians of glacier meadows, in craggy garden nooks full of Nature's darlings. Climb the mountains and get their good tidings. Nature's peace will flow into you as sunshine flows into trees." So wrote John Muir in a famous, much-quoted exhortation.

People had been going to the mountains for self-renewal long before Muir called them, and millions since have found their own personal good tidings under the flawless summer skies of the Sierra. Indeed, as the decades have rolled past, the Sierra has become a vast summer playground.

First of the campers were the goldseekers, whose sprawling encampments, euphemistically called towns, blossomed and died throughout the middle Sierra in the 1850s. The miners were followed by solitary hunters seeking deer and bear, who carried bedroll and tent into the forests. In the 1860s mountaineers began exploring the high country, packing supplies on their backs or on a companionable burro and following game trails up unnamed peaks, along jagged crests, and through steep-walled passes.

Not everyone who sought the "good tidings" heard the same muscular drummer. Pleasure-seekers beelined for mountain resorts as fast as they were opened following the completion of rail and highway connections. Dandies and many-skirted maidens, accompanied by pyramids of Saratoga trunks, headed for Lake Tahoe resorts, which got off to a fast start in the 1860s. Boating, excursions, picnics, lake fishing, and moonlight cruises occupied the jolly habitués. Along with such innocent pastimes, batteries of slot machines, roulette tables, and other games of chance vacuumed money from the imprudent. Thus, the institution of gambling, which took early root, is today well past its centennial.

As an indulgence for a photographer father, a youthful septet lines up along a log in the innocent days of 1907, unimpeded by the Sunday school starch, bubbling over with the spirit of the Sierra summer.

Packing In

Fishing party, outfitted in Abercrombie & Fitch's best, heads
uptrail to a remote lake above Tahoe in 1910. A well-equipped
party such as this usually carried voluminous duffel: heavy canvas
tents, bedrolls, and bulk foods such as flour, corn meal, fresh
vegetables, lard, and a side of bacon. An early grubstake cookbook
specified 170 to 225 pounds of food for four men for a two-week
vacation. Women with the temerity to accompany their men into
the woods (*right*) were expected to wear hot, voluminous riding
habits, topped with bonnets that were forever catching on tree
branches or falling into streams. Those who dared to ride astride
camouflaged their impropriety with billowing layers of skirts.

On the Trail

Trails to high adventure have called hikers to the shining High Sierra ever since John Muir began prowling the mountains with only a sack of tea, some bread, and a blanket. Long before the trails were adequately mapped or marked, inquisitive mountaineers followed the paths worn by game animals, Indians, and sheep, or pioneered new routes through the passes or up the challenging peaks. Sometimes the route was difficult and hazardous, as Stewart Edward White discovered (*right*) in 1904, when he and two others explored an untrodden pass in the southern Sierra. His party crossed treacherous talus slopes, "where a misstep would have tragic consequences" or where "at every stride we stepped ten feet and slid five." Sometimes the route was easy going (*above*), and a man could lash a canoe on the back of a burro and head for glassy tarns that had never before been rippled by a paddle.

However implausible their garb, these four coeds found it no handicap in their mountaineering feats. In 1896 the girls were the first women to descend into Tuolumne Canyon and the third group of women to register their names in the sardine can atop Mount Lyell (elev. 13,095 feet). After climbing the peak, they sat down, "each holding tightly to the one in front. The word was given to let go and zip—in less than a minute we had gone a mile into the softer snow on the lower part of the glacier. The angle at that place is fully 80 degrees." The descent took about three hours; the trip up, seven.

OVERLEAF: Summer pastime for early settlers in the Sierra was hunting bears, which were feared as dangerous nuisances. The bold animals pillaged food stocks, killed livestock, and spooked draft animals. Besides ridding an area of a hazardous pest, hunters received side benefits from a successful bear hunt: bear meat was nourishing, albeit tough and dry; the fur was a source of warm clothing; the fat was "useful for many things, from frying to greasing one's boots." Understandably, the hunters in William Hahn's fine 1882 painting exude an air of quiet self-satisfaction. (From the Kahn Collection, Oakland Museum)

Away at Camp

Resort camping at the turn of the century was a happily cluttered venture. Campers made do with milk cans, apple-box and packing-crate furniture, open-air powder rooms. This is the way Yosemite's Camp Curry looked soon after it opened in 1899. The genial Currys attracted 292 paying guests to their seven-tent resort the first summer.

"A Pleasant Surprise" is the wry title of this letter sheet from Gold Rush days. Bears were as much of a nuisance in the miners' tent colonies as they are today in the National Park campgrounds. Then as now, they helped themselves to the miners' food and rummaged while the campers were away or asleep.

What else is new? Camper-van, photographed in Yosemite in 1921, was built on the chassis of a 1905 Pierce-Arrow. It was fully equipped with all the comforts of home —including draw curtains across the windshield.

Bane of the campers' paradise, mosquitoes attack between April and July up to 10,000 feet. Protection offered in the 1890s: "a not disagreeable" repellent and a bugproof head net.

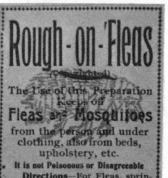

In the earliest years of camping, travelers were often wakened by a coyote shivaree, as suggested in this fanciful drawing of the 1880s.

Tourism in Truckee

On a lazy summer day at Donner Lake in the 1890s, derbied gentlemen in a steam launch and a lonely girl in a rowboat wait for the photographer to finish his time exposure. Donner Lake blossomed into a summer resort in the 1860s soon after completion of the railroad made the lake accessible by stage from Truckee. By 1890 cabins rimmed the shore and a dozen private docks reached out into the water. In this tranquil summer retreat, there was little to remind vacationers of the frightful ordeal that had taken place here only a few years earlier.

For forty years, until it burned in 1935, the curious structure below stood on an eminence overlooking Truckee. A combination home and museum, it was built by an energetic jack-of-all-professions named C. F. McGlashan, who served as a school principal, choral director, newspaper editor and publisher, historian, butterfly collector, and one-man chamber of commerce. He became interested in the hitherto neglected story of the Donner Party and published the first book on the tragedy in 1879. Soon afterward, he built the Grecian pavilion where he kept Donner relics and a butterfly collection. The small pavilion to the right housed a geologic oddity: one of the twenty-five known rocking stones in the world.

A mystery to all who see it, the sixteen-ton, heart-shaped stone stands perfectly balanced on its point in the center of a flat table stone, thirty feet above ground. So delicately poised that a five-year-old child can move it or a strong breeze set it to rocking, the stone still puzzles experts. Was it left behind by a glacier, carried to its lofty perch by aborigines, or patiently chipped away from the base rock by Indians over the centuries? No one knows. A Washoe Indian legend relates that the Wind God placed it there to frighten birds away from the grain and meat that their ancestors dried on the table stone. However it got there, the stone, with its rocker immobilized to prevent vandalism, today stands in a modern steel pavilion, one of Truckee's prime tourist attractions. The Olympic torch burned here for the 1960 Winter Games at Squaw Valley.

High Life at Tahoe

"To obtain the air the angels breathe, you must go to Tahoe," proclaimed brochures for Baldwin's Tallac House, one of the more flamboyant of the dozen luxury resorts that mushroomed around the lake in the seventies and eighties. Boom times in mining and logging, coupled with the opening of trans-Sierra roads and the railroad, brought tourists flocking to the "Lake of the Sky" and established it early as a prime resort area. The Tallac hotel opened on the southwest shore in 1875 as "Yank's" and gained instant fame for its spring-mounted dance floor that made the guests dance "whether they knew or not." The resort was bought in 1881 by an eccentric millionaire, E. J. "Lucky" Baldwin, a man noted for his fondness for fast horses and women. Baldwin renamed the hotel for himself and Mount Tallac, rising behind it, and operated it successfully for twenty-seven years, unabashedly proclaiming it "the Summer Resort of the World," with a "cuisine equal to any, excelled by none." After Baldwin's death in 1908, the resort slowly deteriorated. It was torn down in 1927; only rotting piles now remain.

First of the luxury resorts to open on the west shore, the Grand Central Hotel (1869–95) at Tahoe City advertised black walnut furniture in every room, Brussels carpets, and a cherrywood piano. Rates: $20.00 per week, meals included.

With an air of wicked triumph, "Lucky" Baldwin discomfits his gaming companions with four aces during a round of poker at Tallac in 1900. Gambling came to Tahoe early. Every resort had its casino—Tallac's was the "finest in America" —and though gambling was illegal, enforcement officers were permissive. The imminence of a sheriff's raid was often known hours in advance, allowing ample time to trundle the big round slot machines and gaming tables out of sight.

A Lake of Lapis Lazuli

"Set like a sapphire in a circle of resplendent pearls and opals, lies what is probably the most remarkable and beautiful sheet of water in the world—Lake Tahoe," rhapsodizes an 1890 picture book. "Little steamers furrow this transparent lake, much as a diamond cuts a smooth expanse of glass. Life here is wonderfully exhilarating. The tonic of the mountain air is such that one deep inhalation of its aromatic crispness is like a draught of sparkling wine. Nothing seems wanting to impart to this extraordinary lake the element of the unique: There is a certain mystery in the sad fact, that although many persons have drowned here, no bodies have ever been recovered from deep water. Once gone—they rise no more, but disappear as quietly and effectually as a coin dropped into the sea. One naturally recalls the myths of lovely sirens in their ocean caves, who lured infatuated mortals down to scenes of dazzling splendor, and keep them captives there forevermore." Mark Twain summarized the lake's spell more succinctly: "Three months of camp life on Lake Tahoe would restore an Egyptian mummy to his pristine vigor and give him an appetite like an alligator."

Tahoe's Inland Navy

From 1856 on, the glassy surface of Tahoe has been furrowed by a motley fleet of watercraft, some hauled in on wagons, some built in shoreside ways. The armada carried freight and mail, towed lumber barges or log rafts, circled the shore with excursioners, or ferried boisterous party-goers on moonlight cruises. The imposing *Governor Stanford* (*below*), fourth steamboat on the lake, was launched in 1873 at Lapham. Grossly underpowered, her "one-teakettle boiler" moved her at a snail's pace and she was eventually left behind by her competition. Acknowledged queen of the lake, the opulent *Tahoe* (*right*) was launched in 1896 to a jubilant cacophony of cannon fire and steam whistles. The 196-foot vessel circled the lake for forty years before she was decommissioned. Rather than sell her for scrap, her sentimental owners ordered her scuttled intact in five hundred feet of water in 1940.

A Time for Improvising

Tahoe at the turn of the century was a relaxed retreat, relatively free of the contrivances that stand between a vacationer and contact with nature. The shoreline had not yet become barnacled with piers and sea walls, "No Trespassing" signs were infrequent, and it was possible to walk horses for long distances through the gentle ripples. If the spirit moved you, you could hitch up your clothing, let the shoe float where it would, and wade in to gather pebbles or pollywogs or look for schools of minnows.

In those early years, the snarl of the outboard motor was yet to be heard, water skis yet to be invented. If some Huck Finn wanted to invite two girls and a dog for a boat ride, he had to improvise his own raft and pole his passengers over the shallows. Or, if you did not care about your own neck, you could ride a log towed behind a boat and enjoy a sluggish but foolhardy prelude to water skiing.

When Fish Were Fish

Once the fisherman's utopia, Tahoe yielded tons of the immense Tahoe trout, a delicacy shipped out by the iced carload from 1870 until the early 1900s. Limitless fishing by commercial and sport fishermen so depleted the fish population that the lake was nearly fished out. Nevertheless, there were still some of the big fellows left in the lake when this sun-flecked fisherwoman landed her prize in 1908.

A record catch of eighty silversides, taken in four hours, is displayed outside a resort in 1902. All the resorts retained fishing guides who boated parties to spots where they could virtually swamp the boats with their catch. Resorts held fishing Derbies and awarded prizes for the largest day's catch. The two solemn boys are holding lake cutthroat trout, hooked in 1908.

Up Half Dome with Rope and Toe

be thwarted by the smooth granite rising above them. In 1875 a flock of small boys "who climbed smooth rocks like lizards" got part way up the final ascent and then prudently abandoned the climb.

First mountaineer to conquer Half Dome made it to the top in 1875 (*left*) with ropes and eye-bolts. Simply for the fun of climbing, he nervelessly "drilled his way to the top," reported John Muir, "inserting eye-bolts five or six feet apart, and making his rope fast to each in succession, resting his feet on the last bolt while he drilled a hole for the next above. . . . The whole work was accomplished in a few days." Not to be outdone, Muir clambered up the rope a month later, followed soon by others, among them the first woman to ascend the massif.

"Half Dome never has been, and never will be trodden by human foot," declared the head of the California Geological Survey in the 1860s. Nevertheless, the distinctive monolith in Yosemite Valley was nearly scaled in 1869 by three men who took an Indian escape trail, trusting their lives to bushes and jutting points of rock, and got as far as the top of the lower dome, only to

A permanent cableway was installed up the back of Half Dome in 1927, making the ascent a simple everyday climb—though still a strenuous pull. CCC boys improved the installation (*right*) in the 1930s. The metallic handholds, incidentally, are shunned by knowing climbers when lightning is flickering around the granite peaks.

"Go Climb a Rock"

Following the initial ascents, the challenge of the summits drew mountaineers to the High Sierra, and one lofty peak after another was conquered. By 1890 all the major peaks had been scaled and most of the difficult technical climbs accomplished. Breakthroughs in climbing techniques and specialized equipment cleared the way for climbs of extreme difficulty, such as the historic first ascent of Lost Arrow in Yosemite (*above*) in 1946. Several routes were pioneered up the face of El Capitan (*left*) in the 1950s and 1960s. Climbing the 3,600-foot wall of El Cap took many days of painstaking teamwork in blazing heat or freezing cold, ranging from two and a half days (1952) to an incredible forty-five days (1958) spread over eighteen months. Climbers carried their own water and slept attached like caterpillars to the vertical rock. So popular has rock climbing become that a special school has been established in Yosemite. Its slogan: "Go Climb a Rock."

193

Snow Bound

"The wild, with its brooding silence and mystery, its sadness and laughter; the mountains snow-capped with age-long deposit, the land unequaled in scenic splendor and gorgeous scenery; this will be the supreme treat to the vacationist who will visit the Sierra snowfields this winter." So rhapsodized a railroad brochure in 1916, written to attract people down in the "orange and sunny land" to come up the mountains to play.

For the Sierrans who lived in the higher elevations six months of the year, the exhilaration of playing in the snow was nothing new. As early as 1850 the first ski meets in the country—possibly in the world—were held at Howlands Flat in the northern Sierra, and regular meets were run off and on for thirty years thereafter. During the intervals of glorious clear weather between storms for which the Sierra is famous, winter residents poured out of their houses for tobogganing, sleigh rides, dogsledding, and cross-country and competitive skiing. The deep snowpack gave them access to places that were difficult to reach in summer. On their long skis—known originally as "snow shoes"—they sped across field and valley, over snow-bridged rivers and frozen lakes.

Gradual improvement in winter transportation made the snow sports areas increasingly accessible to outsiders. Rail excursions brought thousands to Norden, Soda Springs, and Truckee before World War I. After the war, a revival of interest in skiing coupled with improvements in equipment attracted more thousands. In the absence of ski resorts, the first skiers were cross-country venturers. Resorts blossomed in the 1930s and 1940s, starved during World War II, and then proliferated after VE Day. The Sierra now has more than a hundred major and minor ski resorts in operation between Thanksgiving and Memorial Day.

A glistening valance of ice, festooning the front of the weathered depot at Truckee, was a familiar sight to the legions of ski fanatics who rode the "Snowball Special" to the Sierra in the 1930s.

Life on Skis

Sierrans living in the deep snows of the mountains adopted the Norwegian ski—then called a "snowshoe"—early in the 1850s. Far more efficient for Sierra use than the clumsy snowshoes of the north woods—which were too awkward and fatiguing to use in the deep snowdrifts and the steep declivities of the Sierra—skis enabled the snowed-ins to get around with relative ease. Strapped to the boots of an athletic and venturesome skier, the eleven-foot slats permitted legendary exploits of cross-country and downhill skiing. Most famous of the cross-country skiers was the phenomenal Snowshoe Thompson (1827–76), a native of Norway, who packed the mail ninety miles over the Sierra between Placerville and Carson City for twenty years beginning in 1856. For a time, he was the sole link between California and the Union during Civil War. In addition to packing the mail, Thompson rescued sick and injured, carried food to snowbound families, delivered medicines and odd cargo such as lamp chimneys, a crystal ball, and a font of newspaper type. He was not the only one to operate a ski-mail service. The "Snow-Shoe Express" (*postmark above*) ran between Downieville and the northern mining camps in the 1850s.

Map of Snowshoe Thompson's incredible postal route. With from fifty to eighty pounds on his back, he would make the eastward journey in three days and return in two. He carried no blankets, relying on exertion to keep him warm.

In the snow country, Sierrans skied from the cradle to the grave. Mourners at a Masonic funeral at La Porte in 1879 park their skis in the snow in front of the church and accompany the casket drawn on a sled. Children were taught to ski almost as soon as they could stand and they were known to zip like weasels through the woods on their outsize skis.

Bundled-up workmen saw blocks of ice from frozen Donner Lake in early 1900s. Ice from Sierra lakes was stored for later use in sawdust-filled icehouses. Some was commercially shipped to inland cities, some was even sent across the Pacific in the holds of steamers.

Out in the Cold

Making the best of a cold world, Sierra residents took advantage of winter's frosty bounty. Frozen lakes became skating rinks, a source for summer ice, or, as above, a means for sledding an office building to a new site. Proficiency in the use of skis in the daily rounds led to afterhour's contests and snow sports and the proliferation of fiercely competitive clubs, such as La Porte's Bar No. 1 (*left*), that often spent as many happy hours at the bar as on the slopes.

The Country's First Ski Meets

First ski competitions in the United States were held in Sierra County in the 1850s by bored Norwegian miners isolated by winter snow. The races involved heavy betting, and quantities of gold dust and coin exchanged hands after every run. Competitors in an 1878 meet (*right*) clown for the photographer at the start of the meet. The course ran two thousand feet downhill from the starting gate at the top, ended where the jumble of skiers is fanning the air.

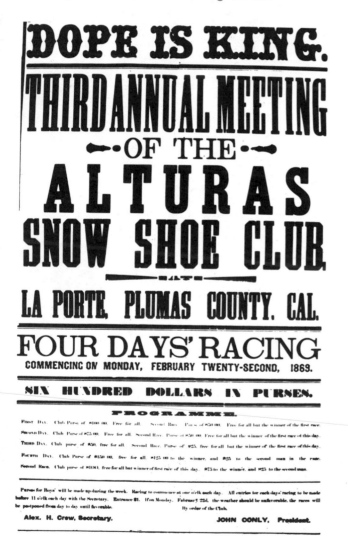

DOPE IS KING.

THIRD ANNUAL MEETING

·OF THE·

ALTURAS

SNOW SHOE CLUB.

LA PORTE, PLUMAS COUNTY. CAL.

FOUR DAYS' RACING

COMMENCING ON MONDAY, FEBRUARY TWENTY-SECOND, 1869.

SIX HUNDRED DOLLARS IN PURSES.

PROGRAMME.

First Day. Club Purse of $100 00. Free for all. Second Race. Purse of $50 00. Free for all but the winner of the first race.

Second Day. Club Purse of $75 00. Free for all. Second Race. Purse of $50 00. Free for all but the winner of the first race of this day.

Third Day. Club purse of $50, free for all. Second Race. Purse of $25, free for all but the winner of the first race of this day.

Fourth Day. Club Purse of $150 00, free for all, $125 00 to the winner, and $25 to the second man in the race. Second Race. Club purse of $100, free for all but winner of first race of this day. $75 to the winner, and $25 to the second man.

Purses for Boys' will be made up during the week. Racing to commence at one o'clk each day. All entries for each days' racing to be made before 11 o'clk each day with the Secretary. Entrance $1. If on Monday, February 22d, the weather should be unfavorable, the races will be postponed from day to day until favorable. By order of the Club.

Alex. H. Crew, Secretary. **JOHN CONLY, President.**

The "dope" referred to above was a noxious-smelling goo that skiers smeared on their "snowshoes" to increase speed. So effective were these mixtures that their formulas were closely guarded secrets. They were generally concocted from whale oil, tars, pitches, waxes, and even a dash of bitters.

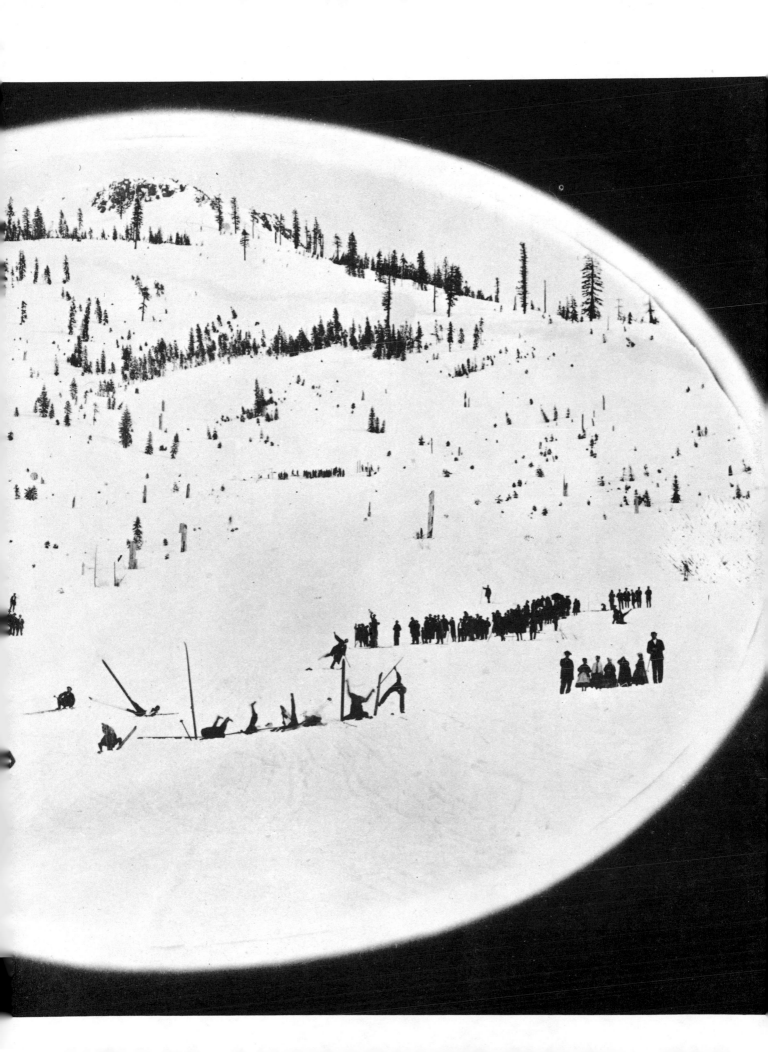

Sizzling Snowshoes

Remarkable 1878 photograph shows the racing technique of the time. Skiers competed in teams down a twenty-five-degree slot. The racers jackknifed on their fourteen-foot skis to reduce wind resistance and thrust a single pole, or "stav," out in front to "cut the air apart." A world's record run on this slope was registered in 1875 by a skier who whistled down at 87.875 miles per hour.

Toasting the winner, a young competitor lifts a glass to a champion racer of the 1890s at La Porte. A team of three (*right*), poised in the starting stance, awaits the gong that will send them flashing down the slope. Racing skis were extra long and heavy, ranging from twelve to fifteen, even twenty-five feet in length. A strong leather strap and a cleat secured them to the high-heeled boots of the "snowshoe artists." The long pole helped skiers uphill, provided balance, and doubled as a brake.

Fiesta of the Snows

A swoop down the toboggan slide attached to Truckee's glistening Ice Palace (1894–1901) was guaranteed to "develop speed sufficient to take the breath away from the most insensate lover of speed." The formidable, icicled roundhouse was built of strong timbers and covered with rabbit wire, which was sprayed nightly to form the shimmering walls, illuminated by twenty arc lights trained on it from the hill above. Within its chilly core, skaters skimmed around a seven hundred-foot oval track to music pumped steaming into the air by fur-coated musicians. The giant building occupied an acre in the middle of Truckee's Main Street, but its ungainly presence was tolerated for the thousands of railroad excursionists that it attracted in winter.

No stretch pants in 1905! The first "snow bunnies" schussed downhill encumbered with layers of flapping skirts.

Prelude to the Ski Boom

Crowds from a "Snowball Special" train converge gingerly on Truckee's Ski Hill in 1932. Few of the excursionists were equipped with skis, for the great skiing boom was just beginning and most of them were content with a day's frolic in the snow. The "Snowball Specials" left San Francisco after midnight and returned just before the next midnight, giving the revelers most of a day in the snowfields. "Wear your old clothes, hiking outfits, or winter sports costumes," counseled the Southern Pacific. "Toss your skiis or other equipment into the baggage car, free of charge." Fare was $4.65 from San Francisco. Breakfast 50 cents, dinner 80 cents, sandwiches a dime. These excursions ran from 1932 until 1940 when they were put out of business by the automobile. Ski resorts opened in the late 1930s along Donner Pass and in Yosemite, and by the early 1940s parking jams such as this all-too-familiar sight at Badger Pass in February 1940 were beginning to be common.

In a heart-stopping duel with gravity, an Olympic contestant sails through the thin air in the eighty-meter jump. Squaw Valley's jumping hill, built in 1959 on Little Papoose Peak, was unique to Olympic facilities, for it combined three separate courses, left to right, the eighty-, sixty-, and forty-meter jumps. Gold medal jump: 306 feet.

Olympic Winter Games VIII

"For the glory of sport and honor of our country," athletes from thirty nations converged on Squaw Valley in 1960 to compete in twenty-seven events staged for the eighth Winter Olympics. A quarter of a million spectators braved winter cold to watch Russian, Scandinavian, German, and Austrian contestants pocket most of the gold medals—with the shining exceptions of individual figure skating and ice hockey, which were resoundingly won by the home team.

Olympic Pageantry

Among the more memorable decorations were heroic, muscular statues, formed of plastic sprayed over a chickenwire form and designed to stand in the fiercest blizzard. Funds for the statues, such as this skater poised in front of Blythe Arena, were donated in advance by California towns that earned the privilege to display them ever after.

Elaborate pageantry, such as this impressive victory ceremony,
marked every stage of the activities. Planned to be "unusual but
within the best of Olympic traditions," the settings and special
effects were produced under Walt Disney's artful direction. More
than fifteen million dollars was invested in creating the Olympic
Village and its sports facilities. Most of the widespread
installation now belongs to the state.

Coming: A Skiers' Utopia?

Major bone of contention is a stretch of highway leading to Mineral King through Sequoia National Park. Point of the debate is whether the Park Service has the legal authority to grant a right-of-way through national parklands for private use and whether the proposed road would endanger the giant sequoias.

Smothered in controversy, a proposed $40-million ski development near Sequoia National Park has embroiled conservationists, government agencies, and a willing developer into a triangular tug-of-war that may persist for years before the issues are resolved. At stake is the conversion of a great natural col at Mineral King (*right*) into an immense skiing complex. Permission was granted to Walt Disney Enterprises to build ski runs and lifts, connecting roads, and an entire alpine village (*above*), but all work was stopped while conservationists and government officials battled in court. Principal challenger has been the Sierra Club, which contends that the government action was illegal and the developer's plans inappropriate. Involved in the lengthy court test is the fundamental question of who determines public policy—government agencies or the public they serve. Meanwhile, the developer bides its time and the skiing public cools its heels.

Mile-High Highways

When the first gasoline buggies sputtered into Yosemite in 1900, their unexpected (and unwanted) arrival announced a new era in Sierra travel. The horse-frightening demons were promptly barred from the park and not admitted until 1913, and then under a battery of restrictions, but motor cars soon began to poke their radiators into other parts of the Sierra. In 1906 an intrepid woman driver made the front page by coaxing a chain-driven Simplex from Sacramento to Tahoe in only eight hours! The rush was on.

Early motorists who ventured into the Sierra had to make do with roads that were barely negotiable for wagons. The Sonora Pass road, according to the Highway Department in 1901, offered "22 miles over granite formation that is little more than a creek bed." Roads were so dusty in summer and muddy in winter that one highway was described as "130 miles long and 5 feet deep."

Motor cars, being far more delicate than Missouri mules, required all-weather routes, hard surfaces, and service stops along the way. To accommodate the growing legion of "wheelmen," the state slowly began improving the main mountain roads, starting in 1909. However, the modest budgets were usually consumed in repairing winter damage—the Lake Tahoe road required all but nine cents of its bridge funds in 1908 for repairs—and no money was left for new construction. Road building costs were exorbitant, the season brief, and the volume of traffic so meager that highway funds were diverted to populous areas where the proliferating automobile was running amok. Even today, only three of the trans-Sierra passes meet interstate highway specifications, and segments of the other five are still engineered to the leisurely, eight-mile-a-day pace of wagon and stage.

Runabout pauses in 1910 on a hairpin turn on Meyers Grade, a road that had changed little since its completion in 1860. For many years this route was the only trans-Sierra road suitable for motor cars until the regrading of Sonora Pass in 1912. The Tahoe road was the first official state highway (1896).

Highway Hucksters

Five flag-bedecked Studebakers—the last one a rolling garage with spare tires, parts, and tools—belonged to the Inyo Good Road Club, a touring group dedicated to promoting a scenic highway loop as part of the 1915 Panama-Pacific Exposition. The five-car caravan circled the state in 1913, passed through Walker Pass (*above*), then little more than a game trail, and detoured into Yosemite. The club hoped to generate financial support for the proposed highways, which at that time were supported by a mixture of state, federal, county, and even private capital. Toll roads, built by private funds, operated in the Sierra as late as 1917.

Terrifying Tioga

"It is not unusual," commented the A.A.A., "to find people who just go to pieces, freeze at the wheel, and park their cars in the middle of the road to wait for the Park Ranger or a kindly motorist to drive their cars the rest of the way." This notorious road, which terrified motorists from the day of its opening as a through route in 1915 to its final realignment in 1961, was actually two roads spliced together. The first, known as the Great Sierra Wagon Road, was built in 1882–83 eastward from Crocker's station, near the present boundary of Yosemite, to a short-lived mining community near the summit of Tioga Pass. The second portion, built westward up a steep canyon from Lee Vining, was not completed until 1909, by which time the old mining road had become nearly impassable. The two roads were purchased in 1915, repaired, and opened to through traffic.

Certain portions of the Tioga Road have left scars in the memories of two generations of motorists, notably, the steep grade to Lee Vining, "just a fraction more than one-car wide with an unfenced drop-off of as much as two thousand feet," and a twenty-one-mile remnant of the 1883–1961 mining road, sourly recalled for its narrowness, its twisting path among trees and boulders, and its roller-coaster roadbed. Unbelievably, this tortuous route was once proposed for a trans-Sierra railroad right-of-way. A company was financed in 1882 and a survey was completed, but no tracks were ever laid.

Hollywood Finds the Pass

A cameraman cranks away in a canoe in 1925, filming a James Oliver Curwood story on the shore of Lyons Dam reservoir, a reasonable facsimile of a North Woods lake a few miles from Sonora Pass. More pictures have been filmed in the Sonora area than any other locality outside of Hollywood. The three-hundred-plus films produced here since 1915 include dozens of westerns, featuring Tom Mix and William S. Hart, *The Perils of Pauline,* several *Rose Maries,* and the complete adventures of Lassie. A column of Falangist tanks and troop carriers (*right*) rumbles down Sonora Pass on its way to disaster near Dardanelle in a climactic scene (filmed from the top of a pine tree) in *For Whom the Bell Tolls,* shot here in 1941 and 1942.

Road Building—a Job for Mountain Goats

Road builders, blasting and bulldozing their way across the granite summits of the Sierra, face many of the same problems that beset the section gangs that chipped a path for the Central Pacific a century earlier. Even with heavy equipment and powerful explosives, the crews can only work the four months between snowfalls, wrestling ponderous earthmoving equipment on narrow ledges. Gangs working in the shade, even in summer, are chilled by the cold, which interferes with the setting of paving mixtures, and must handle explosives with great precision so that the blasting does not block the access roads. Tunnels, cuts, fills, bridges, and balustrades challenge their engineering skills and bring out the mountain goat in the men. Through all this muscular turmoil, convoys of rubber-necking tourists have to be briskly shepherded.

420-7

Clearing Super Snowfalls

Barely visible in a twenty-foot trench of snow, a rotary methodically chews its way over Donner Summit in 1952 in a vain effort to open U. S. 40. Succeeding storms blocked the pass for five more weeks, the longest period of traffic interruption since the introduction of modern snow-clearing equipment. Ordinarily, half of the Sierra passes are kept open in winter, but once in a while a super snowfall seals them all. Cannon fire (*left*) knocks down cornices before they can build up into avalanches that would destroy settlements or smash into highway traffic. Even cleared roads (*right*) are sometimes edged with walls of snow that loom above the largest trucks.

The Excesses of Spring

"Watch for rocks!" admonishes the roadside sign, and once in a great while, something really impressive rolls down, such as this immense boulder that blocked U. S. 40 near Meyers in 1952. The odds against such a happenstance are probably a million to one, but less spectacular rockslides are commonplace in wet winters or periods of heavy spring run-off. Rocks are most likely to come loose at night when ice forms around or under them and forces them from their beds. Heavy rainfall also produces localized floods that scour out highways (*above*), undermine trestle footings, or flood canyons such as Yosemite Valley, which sometimes fills wall-to-wall with icy water for a day or two.

Wings Over the Crest

For speed enthusiasts, who found highway travel over the Sierra too slow, the prospect of flying across the Sierra crest has had great appeal. As early as 1849, visionary promoters were booking tickets for flights to the gold fields in "aerial locomotives" powered by steam engines that would carry from fifty to one hundred passengers at from sixty to one hundred miles per hour, "among or above the clouds." En route, travelers would "find themselves waving to the western breeze and conversing by the way with merry farmers in the fields of broom and grain." Idyllic as this may have sounded, actual crossing of the Sierra by air did not occur until 1911. Experimental glider flights were conducted near Luther Pass in the 1890s, but the first attempted airplane crossings in the early 1900s met with disaster. The underpowered planes, operating in the rarefied air, could neither gain the needed altitude nor cope with the turbulent air currents, a deadly combination that even modern pilots of light planes respect and fear.

First pilot to attempt to fly across the Sierra, Bob Fowler, headed for Donner
Pass in 1911—and was blown right back. The two hundred-pound,
Wright-built biplane was not powerful enough to break through the gusty
winds, which flipped it on its back and sent it crashing into the trees near
Colfax. Fowler tumbled down through the branches and miraculously escaped
serious injury. Even more miraculously, the wrecked plane (*left*) was patched
together in ten days. The pilot made three more attempts to cross the pass, but
his plane could not climb high enough. He gave up, flew south to Los Angeles
and crossed the San Gabriel Range by a low-level route. He was competing
for a $50,000 prize for the first transcontinental flight to be completed in
thirty days. He made it to New York, but lost the prize because the trip took
forty-five days (and sixty-six landings).

The First Sierra Birdmen

First man successfully to fly over Mount Whitney, Silas Christofferson, made it
on the second try in June 1914, taking off from Bishop on the east side of
the peak. On the first attempt, he was accompanied by a photographer, who,
seated on the gasoline tank, cranked away with a movie camera. The pair
had ascended to ten thousand feet, with saw-toothed peaks and steep-walled
canyons below, when crosscurrents caught the plane and wrenched it into a
nose dive. The pilot wrestled the rickety craft back to level flight after a
whistling descent of 1,800 feet and landed safely. Understandably, the shaken
cameraman declined to accompany him on his second, and successful, flight
two days later.

One of the earliest—perhaps *the* earliest—single-wing airplane stands in front of a hangar at the Grass Valley Aerodrome, claimed to be the first commercial field in the country and the first airport in the West, opened in 1908.

"The man who robbed the eagle of his secret," diffident Lyman Gilmore, working in the obscurity of the Sierra, pioneered a number of aviation firsts that are just beginning to be recognized. In the 1890s he experimented with glider flight at Big Meadows in El Dorado County. About 1895 he started designing a cabin-type monoplane with retractable landing gear and aluminum wing covering. In 1902 he built and flew a thirty-two-foot glider with a twenty-horsepower steam engine—a year before the Wright brothers' historic flight. His plane made more than twenty successful flights from one hundred yards to a mile or more under perfect control. There is a school named in his honor in Grass Valley.

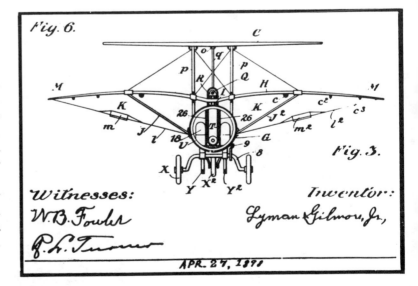

Air Force Discovers Yosemite

A three-winged bombing plane over Yosemite? In this puzzle picture, there are actually two planes, Martin medium bombers, flying so close together that the camera records them as one in this photograph from the late twenties. Military flights over National Parks are now restricted to above two thousand feet. Present-day visitors to Yosemite, who wince at the sonic booms that today's Navy jet pilots delight in slamming against Yosemite's echoing granite, may have reason to wonder if this restriction is still in force—or enforced.

First plane to land in Yosemite, piloted by an Army lieutenant, touched down May 27, 1919. Second landing occurred at Wawona in December 1923.

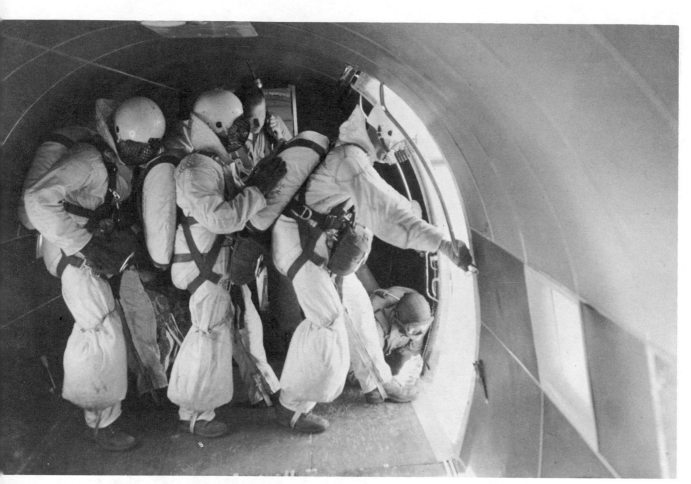

Getting the Drop on Fire

Essentially a military-type operation, forest fire suppression depends on military hardware and equipment. Helitack crewmen, protected with specially designed suits, parachute into remote, roadless areas to control small fires before they get out of hand. Vintage bombing planes, adapted to discharge thousands of gallons of fire-quenching chemicals, lay down firebreaks ahead of the path of the flames. (Such efficiency has improved the fire suppression rate, but caused some ecologists to warn that overcontrol of forest fires may in the long run damage the forest ecosystem—a contention that the Sierra Club has been advancing since 1905.)

The Crowded Crystal Ball

"Mount Whitney, the second tallest mountain in the nation, is gaining a dubious reputation as America's highest trash can," commented a news dispatch in 1970. The story further reported that the twenty thousand hikers who scrambled to the top of the peak that year left behind tons of paper, bottles, cans, and other reminders of the world below that had to be hauled out by packtrains and helicopters.

This unhappy picture is not unique to Mount Whitney. People-pressure is everywhere in evidence in the Sierra. Portions of the John Muir Trail have been worn out by the passage of thousands of boots and hoofs, and miles have been closed or rerouted. Trails through meadows have turned to trenches and become eroded into gullies. In some areas hikers have burned all the down wood for campfires and chopped branches off living trees; packtrains have grazed off all the grass. Once-pure tarns are now polluted: Smog has choked Yosemite Valley on crowded weekends and has forced the closing of fire lookouts in the Tahoe Basin because observers could no longer spot forest fire smoke in the dense haze.

Attempts to control the crush of people are being implemented. The number of camp sites are being reduced and the duration of campers' visits limited in the National Parks and Forests. The National Parks are gradually phasing out the automobile. Packers' associations and the Sierra Club are packing smaller groups into less frequented areas. Planning agencies in the mountain counties are beginning to say No to real estate developers.

The day will come when even more drastic controls will be needed. Vast as it is, the Sierra offers only a limited amount of accessible recreational area, and its proper use will be the challenging concern of the government and an enlightened public for decades to come.

No room at the top. Resting climbers crowd the summit of lofty Mount Whitney. So great is the need for people to escape the urban scene that increasing thousands are hiking the Sierra trails each summer.

237

ACKNOWLEDGMENTS

Tracking down pictorial material for this book has been rewarding because of personal contacts with collectors and curators. Some sixty individuals have contributed to the book. To these helpful and generous people, I wish to convey the deepest gratitude.

In addition to those listed below, I would specially like to thank the following: Harold G. Schutt, for his generous loan of materials; Larry Nahm and Bill Jones of the National Park Service for guidance in the Yosemite Research Library; to Philip Palmer, of Sequoia-Kings Canyon National Park, for access to the photographic archives; to Dan Gridley of the Sierra Club for help in selecting photographs from the club's historical collection; to Peter Evans, Librarian of the California Historical Society, for making available the Schmiedel collection; to George Kraus of the Southern Pacific for access to the company's albums; to Lee Sherwood of the Western Pacific for archival materials on the line's crossing the range; and to Bud Scott of Pebble Beach for counsel on Tahoe history and permission to re-run photographs from his book about the Lake in the Sky.

Thanks to the San Mateo County Historical Society for information about early airplane crossings of the Sierra; to Shirley Sargent, for the loan of the fine Theodore S. Solomons photograph of the Sweet sisters; to Roy Baker and members of the Truckee-Donner Historical Society for information about Truckee's early days; to Nona Quill for information about her grandfather, the remarkable C. F. McGlashan; to Henry H. Clifford for arranging for reprinting of the Henry Van Winkle photo published in the Los Angeles Corral *Brand Book;* to Leavitt Dudley for ferreting out production shots from *For Whom the Bell Tolls;* to Aletha Rae and Norman Wilson for assistance on the pages devoted to State Historical Monuments; to Bob Krieger of the Division of Highways for early highway photos; and to Florence Williams of Three Rivers for information on Captain Charles Young.

No California pictorial would be possible without the assistance of Allan Ottley and his staff at the California State Library, Irene Simpson Neasham and her knowledgeable crew at the Wells Fargo Bank History Room, and the ever-helpful John Barr Tompkins at Bancroft Library.

Special appreciation is expressed to George R. Stewart, Richard Dillon, Harold C. Bradley; and to Francis P. Farquhar, for encouragement and for making available the photographs he gathered for his classic *History of the Sierra Nevada.*

PHOTO CREDITS

(Abbreviations: T — top; B — bottom; L — left; R — right.)
Kramer Adams, *Logging Railroads of the West:* 132, 142, 143.
California Historical Society, San Francisco: 12, 28T, 35T, 98T, 118, 141, 162, 163, 168, 170, 171, 172B, 177B, 186, 187, 188, 189B, 198T, 205B, 231T.
California State Archives, Sacramento: 49B, 59B, 60, 177C.
California State Division of Parks and Recreation, Sacramento: 15, 16, 27BL, 28B, 30, 32, 33, 35B, 36, 41, 42T, 44B, 45, 46, 47, 48, 49T, 51, 112B, 176B, 178T, 179, 199, 200, 204, 205T, 208, 209.
California State Division of Highways, Sacramento: 14, 216, 217T, 219, 222L, 223, 224, 225, 226.
California State Library, Sacramento: 26B, 44T, 50, 52, 53, 56B, 80, 95, 96T, 196T, 197, 198B, 201, 202, 203, 217B, 228, 229.
E. B. Crocker Art Gallery, Sacramento: 102–103.
Denver Public Library, Western Division: 8.
Esquire Magazine, painting by Harper Goff: 79.
Luggi Foeger, Incline Village: 210.
Frasher Fotos, Pomona: 160–161.
Grass Valley-Nevada City *Union:* 231B.
Henry E. Huntington Library, San Marino: 34.
Forrest Jackson, Modesto: 6–7.
Russ Johnson, Bishop: 230.
Joslyn Art Museum, Omaha, Nebraska: 66–67.
John Morrell & Co., Chicago: 29.
National Park Service, Sequoia-Kings Canyon National Park, Three Rivers: 11, 126B, 136, 154, 155.
National Park Service, Yosemite National Park: 18, 20, 21, 92, 94, 96B, 97, 99B, 100, 101, 104, 105, 106B, 107, 108, 119, 144, 152, 153, 157, 158, 159B, 177T, 190, 191, 206, 222B, 227, 232, 233.
Native Sons of the Golden West, San Francisco: 1.
Nevada Historical Society, Reno: 139.
Oakland Art Museum: 31, 122–123, 174–175.
Leigh Ortenburger, Palo Alto: 193.
Pacific Gas and Electric Co., San Francisco: 42B.
Paramount Pictures, Inc., Hollywood: 220B, 221.
Gene Rose, courtesy of the Fresno *Bee:* 236.
San Francisco *Examiner:* 86–87.
San Francisco Water and Power Department: 164, 165.
Shirley Sargent, Yosemite, photograph by Theodore Solomons: 173.
Edward B. Scott, *The Saga of Lake Tahoe:* 27BR, 131T, 181, 183, 185, 189T, 214.
Harold G. Schutt, Lindsay: 10, 114L, 114B, 115, 116, 117, 124, 126T, 127, 130, 131B, 133T, 134, 135, 137, 138, 140B.
The Sierra Club, San Francisco, photographs by J. N. LeConte: 2–3, 147, 150–151, 159T.
Southern Pacific Railroad, San Francisco: 25, 43, 59T, 61, 62, 72, 75, 76, 77, 78, 81, 82, 83, 84–85, 180B, 184, 194, 207.
Truckee-Donner Historical Society, Truckee: 74T, 179T.
United States Forest Service, San Francisco: 234, 235.
University of California, Bancroft Library: 13, 26–27T, 40, 56T, 57, 71, 99T, 110, 111, 112T, 113, 114T, 120, 121, 128, 133B, 140T, 146, 148, 149, 172T, 220.
University of Calif. Library, Berkeley: 106L, 166, 167.
Walt Disney Productions, Burbank: 212, 213.
Wells Fargo Bank History Room, San Francisco: 38–39, 54, 58, 64, 65, 68, 69, 70, 196.
The Westerners, Los Angeles Corral, *Brand Book No. 9:* 63.
Western Pacific Railroad, San Francisco: 88, 89, 90, 91.
A. F. Worthington, Truckee: 22.
William Young, San Francisco: 211.
Yosemite Park & Curry Co., Yosemite: 176T, 192, 218.

INDEX

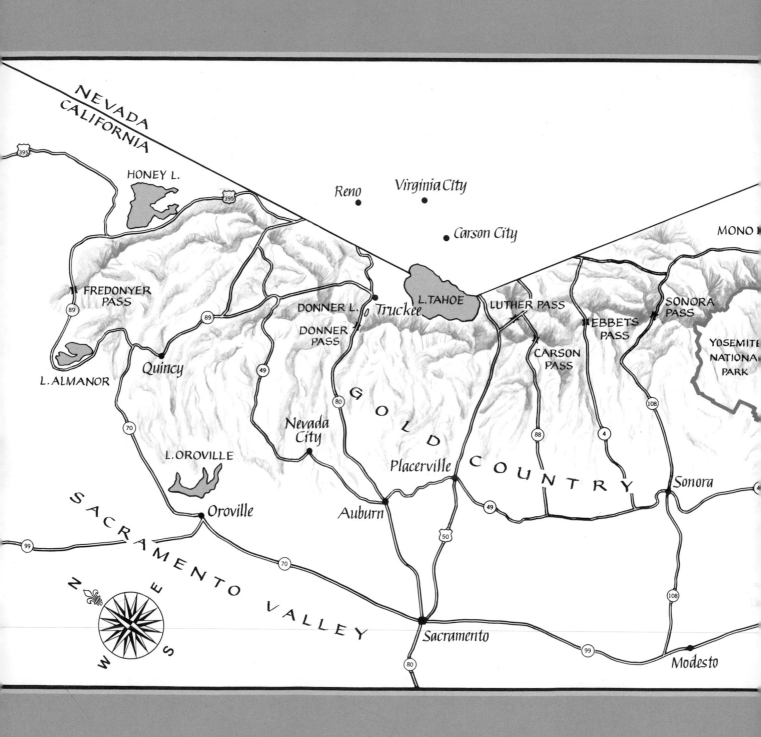